The Elements (and Pleasures) of Difficulty

The Elements of Composition Series

Series Editor: William A. Covino, Florida Atlantic University

David Blakesley
The Elements of Dramatism

Edward P. J. Corbett and Rosa A. Eberly
The Elements of Reasoning, Second Edition

William A. Covino
The Elements of Persuasion

Catherine L. Hobbs
The Elements of Autobiography and Life Narratives

Elizabeth McMahan, Robert Funk, and Susan Day
The Elements of Writing about Literature and Film

Thomas E. Pearsall
The Elements of Technical Writing, Second Edition

Mariolina Rizzi Salvatori and Patricia Donahue
The Elements (and Pleasures) of Difficulty

Heidi Schultz
The Elements of Electronic Communication

William Strunk, Jr., and E. B. White
The Elements of Style, Fourth Edition

Bradford T. Stull
The Elements of Figurative Language

The Elements (and Pleasures) of Difficulty

Mariolina Rizzi Salvatori

University of Pittsburgh

Patricia Donahue

Lafayette College

New York San Francisco Boston
London Toronto Sydney Tokyo Singapore Madrid
Mexico City Munich Paris Cape Town Hong Kong Montreal

To our husbands
Romano Salvatori and
Michael Garst

Vice President and Publisher: Eben W. Ludlow
Marketing Manager: Wendy Albert
Production Manager: Ellen MacElree
Project Coordination, Text Design, and Electronic Page Makeup: Electronic Publishing Services Inc., NYC
Cover Designer/Manager: John Callahan
Manufacturing Manager: Mary Fischer
Printer and Binder: R. R. Donnelley and Sons Company
Cover Printer: Coral Graphic Services

For permission to use copyrighted material, grateful acknowledgment is made to the copyright holders on p. 177, which is hereby made part of this copyright page.

Library of Congress Cataloging-in-Publication Data

Salvatori, Mariolina Rizzi.
The elements (and pleasures) of difficulty / Mariolina Rizzi Salvatori, Patricia Donahue.
p. cm. -- (The elements of composition series)
Includes index.
ISBN 0-321-10617-2
1. English language--Rhetoric--Handbooks, manuals, etc. 2. Literature--History and criticism--Theory, etc.--Handbooks, manuals, etc. 3. Meaning (Philosophy) in literature--Handbooks, manuals, etc. 4. Readability (Literary style)--Handbooks, manuals, etc. 5. Criticism--Authorship--Handbooks, manuals, etc. 6. Academic writing--Handbooks, manuals, etc. I. Donahue, Patricia, 1953- II. Title. III. Series.
PE1479.C7S25 2005
808--dc22
2004022899

Please visit us at http://www.ablongman.com.

ISBN 0-321-10617-2

2 3 4 5 6 7 8 9 10—DOH—07 06 05

Contents

Preface for Instructors

> Teaching is even more difficult than learning. We know that; but we rarely think about it. And why is teaching more difficult than learning? Not because the teacher must have a larger store of information, and have it always ready. Teaching is more difficult than learning because what teaching calls for is this: to let learn. The real teacher, in fact, lets nothing else be learned than—learning...The teacher is ahead of his apprentices in this alone, that he has still far more to learn than they—he has to learn to let them learn. The teacher must be capable of being more teachable than the apprentices.
>
> —*Martin Heidegger*

We are pleased you have chosen to consider and even work with our **textbook.** In this Preface, we want to share with you some of the thinking that is behind its inception and development. We understand that at first glance this book may look different from other textbooks you have used. It revisits the philosophical idea that "difficulty" can be "understood." It does so by shifting the investigation to some of the difficulties students experience with certain texts, and it suggests that these difficulties can be explored in elemental terms. Thus, it contains long passages of student writing that it mines for ideas, content, ways of understanding. Although it focuses on reading, this book is also about writing: It assumes the importance of teaching both reading and writing in the college-level curriculum—reading in the composition classroom and writing in the literature classroom—a combination that is often avoided because one process, and the approach to teaching it, seems to interfere with the other.

In addition, this book emerges out of and reflects our commitment to the principles and practices of what is variously called "student-centered learning," "active learning," or "self-reflexive pedagogy." And insofar as this movement has been so influential in education, we assume many of you will find this book more familiar (and congenial) than it might at first appear. At its heart is a particular kind of classroom encounter, one we have experienced and think you probably have as well.

Revisiting a Classroom Scene

Imagine this scene. You enter your classroom full of enthusiasm and eager to initiate discussion about a piece of writing—a poem, a play, an essay, an autobiography, a newspaper article. Soon you realize that nothing much is taking place. Your students seem reluctant to contribute. Then one volunteers that the material was "boring," another that he "didn't understand it." What do you do?

If you are like most teachers, on such occasions (and despite your best intentions), you may find yourself relying on certain default strategies, which have worked before in similar situations. Or you may instinctively do what some of your own teachers did and what most of your students expect you to do: you resolve your students' confusion didactically by explaining passages, explaining **meanings**, defining unclear terms. When you leave the classroom, you may very well share this experience with a colleague, who not only might relate back to you a similar experience, but also assign responsibility for *what did not happen* to students. As you walk toward your office, however, and in your mind revisit the classroom scene, you begin to sense that you could have handled the situation differently. You know that one student could not relate to the material. Another did not understand it. But you do not know why. You begin to realize that in your desire to model for your students how to read, you have actually prevented yourself from paying attention to what they were saying. Now you wish you could have handled the situation differently—wish you could have turned the problem back onto the students. You wish you could have guided them in confronting it head on. But how? What kinds of questions to ask? What kind of writing to assign?

We do not want to mislead you. This book is not a panacea, nor is it a collection of "teaching tips." And since it is a book that approaches these questions in ways that you may be unaccustomed to, let us first consider what this book is not.

What This Book Is Not

- Even though it refers to, but is not limited to, several so-called "literary" genres, it is not an introduction to literary analysis. (Many such books already exist, and our book would work nicely alongside them.) Its purpose is not to provide students with information about literary conventions, tropes, and terms, but to encourage them to reflect on and articulate the knowledge they already possess about language, texts, reading, and writing.
- Even though it includes examples of published texts, it is not an anthology or a reader in the typical sense. It can serve, however, as a welcome accompaniment to such materials by making explicit the challenges they present.
- Even though it refers to theorists and theoretical terms, it is not an introduction to theory *per se*. It mentions particular historical and literary figures and offers brief summaries of their ideas, not only to encourage students to read further, but also to make visible the theoretical influences that often remain unidentified in what teachers and students say. It unpacks a great deal of **academic nomenclature** because underneath such terms is a mountain of knowledge that whoever selected a term first had to identify and analyze.
- Even though it focuses on what is called **close reading,** it is not a book wedded to the theoretical school (formalism) from which the approach evolved. It does, however, help students to read closely and bring to light the "formalist" assumptions about texts they have acquired in previous work, so they can complicate those assumptions, challenge them, build on them.
- Even though it is a book that examines various *products*—academic, literary, social—its emphasis is on *process*—reading and writing as processes of identifying and **negotiating** difficulty, learning as a process of systematic self-reflection. As a book about process, it initiates work, but it expects teachers and students to complete such work together.

What This Book Is and Does

- This is a book that figures the student as a reader to be taken seriously.

- This is a book that looks at complicated issues of reading, writing, and interpretation directly inside the work of students as they confront and work to negotiate difficult texts.
- This is a book that makes extensive use of students' writing, valuing it for what it is as opposed to what it is not.
- This is a book that presents the identification (description and naming) of difficulty as an important precursor to understanding, and it encourages students to see those moments in their reading when they feel stymied or confused as gateways rather than barriers to understanding.
- This is a book that enables a teacher not only to classify and be ready to work with the general types of difficulties students bring with them (or generate), but also the specific challenges posed by certain genres, discourses, and academic conventions.

Why We Wrote This Book

We would like to share with you how we came to embrace difficulty. Our ideas about difficulty emerged from many years of actual classroom work with undergraduates struggling to make sense of difficult texts in composition and literature classes, and also with graduate students exploring questions of teaching and learning in seminars in pedagogy, teaching of composition, and courses in theories of reading (hermeneutics, reception theories, reader response). One of us has taught for many years in a large public state university, the other in a highly selective liberal arts college. Yet, despite the differences in our students' educational background and degree of preparation (one might ask, "prepared" for what?), our students often responded to confusion in the same way: They placed it beyond their ability to negotiate, whether they located it *in* the text or *in* themselves.

Gradually and independently of each other at first, we noticed that despite our efforts to situate student learning at the center of our pedagogical praxis, whenever students expressed confusion we believed it our responsibility to step in and clarify it. That is what we had seen many of our teachers do when we were students. It is what we had been told needed to be done when we were younger teachers. And it is an approach that colleges and universities perpetuate and reward.

But an educational enterprise that positions teachers as all-knowing and students as not-knowing is one in which students (particularly undergraduates) rarely learn to tackle difficulties on their own. It is simply easier, and more efficient, for a teacher to resolve these problems herself, even if by doing so she encourages dependency and passivity. It is because difficulties are indeed an intrinsic aspect of understanding that students need to be taught to think about them. They need to be provided with opportunities to consider the effect of what Hans-Georg Gadamer calls **"prejudices"** or **"pre-understandings"**—that is, the sediments of prior judgments and understandings that inevitably affect, sometimes positively, sometimes negatively, and mostly darkly, the judgments we presently issue, the understandings we form. And, thus, this book.

What Are the Challenges of Our Approach?

We want to acknowledge that there are several challenges that teachers new to this approach might experience. First, the tools we propose are meant only for **propedeutic,** preparatory work. And with a few exceptions, the samples of student writing are not from final, polished papers, but represent work in progress. They are responses to "assisted invitations" (the I.A. Richards' term that Ann Berthoff brought to life in composition studies) to develop and to adopt reflexive habits of mind that will serve them well in their college studies as well as in daily life. The work initiated here, therefore, must be completed by you and your students.

But what does it mean to define the work with difficulty as preparatory. For what? It can be work that prepares students to understand how reflection works, so they can more fully understand how they think (at least about certain subjects), how they formulate ideas, their weight, their consequences. It can be work that demonstrates to students what is communal about the way they think. It can be work that leads to writing essays in which students, having mined specific difficulties, move from that private moment of understanding to public articulation, to generalization and theory-making. Teachers may want to decide the final "product," which can be a research, or argumentative, expository, or creative essay. Or they may want to guide students toward the format that would best enable them to bring their inquiry to fruition.

Second, we want to acknowledge that some readers may suspect that in reading student texts the way we do we are actually "reading into" them, constructing their difficulties as moments of understanding when those difficulties are really only markers of error, of things improperly done. Indeed, in our approach to teaching, we are committed to mining—and to encouraging our students to mine—the knowledge they, as students, bring to the classroom. And that includes the knowledge that (according to dominant criteria) produces erroneous understandings. Not to do so, we think, is to declare that knowledge as irrelevant and unworthy. So, yes, we do *read into* student texts, the same way we read into established literary texts, with similar pleasure, and for similar reasons: looking for clues, directions, signs of work begun. When students realize that their teachers ask the same questions of student texts that they ask of the texts they have assigned for class reading, and when they understand that those questions are asked not to punish or to slight them, but to foreground their work of reading, they begin to take tremendous pride and great pleasure in this kind of inquiry.

Through this "close reading" of student texts, we have repeatedly discovered that what students perceive as moments of difficulty can be understood differently: as moments when they, guided by internalized theories of reading they do not control, read a text in ways that inhibit even the consideration of an alternative. The student writing that records these readings tends to be marked by vehement expressions, unwavering conclusions, or a tendency toward premature closure. But when these moments are opened to reflection through appropriate questions (Why do you think so? What assumptions about "X" guide your evaluation of this text? What assumptions about reading and writing lead you to assume that punctuation rules cannot be broken?), they reveal what they would seem to cover over: insights into ways of thinking that students sense the text is pressuring them to entertain but that they are not quite ready to follow through on. These moments of difficulty are worth exploring.

Finally, we should tell you that students may find difficulty a puzzling concept at first. Interestingly, the students who are most unsure of their reading abilities may be the first to benefit from the approach. The Difficulty Paper Assignment validates their difficulties and readily produces startling work. But you may also hear the following objections: "How can we name a difficulty while we are having difficulty to begin with?" Or, "What's the point of analyzing a difficulty when once we do it ceases to be a difficulty?" Other students, especially those so-called "good" students who have been rewarded for representing themselves as knowledgeable, may say they cannot find anything difficult in what they are reading. And yet other students may be hesitant to identify what might be difficult because they feel embarrassed, or ashamed, as if the identification of difficulty were an indictment of their abilities. We urge you to be sensitive to such different responses and to understand them. Do not be discouraged. Keep providing different students with different opportunities to explore the meaning of their difficulties and to bring their underlying assumptions to the fore. This is the work that only you can do for and with your students. A textbook can only make suggestions and give certain directions. But it is teachers like you that can make students "get it." And it is our experience that once students "get it," they, like their teachers, find such work valuable and liberating, pleasurable and intellectually fulfilling.

How This Book Is Organized

Our book is divided into seven chapters, with an "Intermezzo" separating the work of the first three chapters from the remaining three. In the first three chapters, we introduce the notion of difficulty, examine the difficulties presented by lyric poetry, and follow that with a chapter on reading *The Rime of the Ancyent Marinere,* a text that is poetic, but long, and also contains several narrative elements. The fourth chapter, the "Intermezzo," is meant to create a bridge between our work on poetry and prose and also to provide an example of a detailed inquiry into one reader's difficulties. So often, courses in reading and writing, first-year composition, and introductions to literature examine student writing less for what it says than how it says it (or what it does not say). We hope this chapter will demonstrate the richness in understanding that student writing offers both teachers and other students.

Chapter 4 also makes what you might consider an unexpected move. It deliberately blocks access to the text (Carolyn Steedman's *Landscape for a Good Woman*) the student is responding to. We do so to divert attention from Steedman and spotlight the reading moves of Susan Connelly, the student whose work we examine. We believe Connelly has a lot to teach all of us about reading, reflexivity, self-examination, and revision. Paying close attention to students' moves, particularly when they seem belabored or counterintuitive, may enable teachers to remember some of the fundamental reading difficulties they learned to solve long ago and are now blind to. Remembering those difficulties may make teachers more sensitive to their students' difficulties. In the three chapters that follow this "middle," we examine difficulties offered by prose narrative, the personal essay, and certain academic constructions, such as Michel Foucault's "author function." In every chapter, we make ample use of students' writing about difficulty, since it is those texts that provided the source material for this book. Our intent is to demonstrate that even if they are not familiar with theoretical articulations of the fundamental concepts of our discipline, students often read and write as if they already knew them, at times enacting them, at times calling them into question.

Finally, in each chapter we introduce certain theoretical terms. Our purpose is to show how students' work foreshadows or reflects the subject matter of critical theories and also to provide students with a language for refining their emerging conceptualizations. Each chapter concludes with two brief sections: in "Taking Stock," students reflect on what they have done; in "Retrospective," chapters are summarized to provide for conceptual scaffolding.

How You Can Use This Book

We imagine this book being used in different ways, in different kinds of courses. Since it is a slim volume, it could easily supplement or sit aside other texts on reading and interpretation, texts suitable for work in introductory and advanced literature and theory courses, and writing courses that emphasize reading. We also imagine this book being useful to graduate students in courses on pedagogy, as a way for them to think about the theoretical elements of teaching and the relationship between reading and writing.

Although this book is not a reader as such, the Appendices include several excerpts of the literary texts discussed here, as well as several poems. In the case of two older texts that are in the public domain (Coleridge's *The Rime of the Ancyent Marinere* and Montaigne's "Of Books" from his *Essais*), students are referred to web sites where these texts can be found. Students may also conduct their own searches, under your guidance. In that sense, then, the book is self-contained. Our intent here is to begin to prepare students for the work that all of us do when we read texts that comment on or refer to texts we have not read and access only through quotations. But a teacher may very well decide that she wants her students to read in their entirety the texts our students responded to. In that case, the teacher can assign them. She can intervene in the structure of the book and adjust it to her own needs. If a teacher chooses not to use those texts, other materials will serve just as well.

The chapters in this book have been written to be read in chronological order, with later chapters building on, and at times complicating, the work of earlier ones. But a teacher could easily choose to teach the chapters in a different order or use the general list of difficulties presented in the "Retrospective" section as an organizational guideline. It is even possible to create several different kinds of pathways through this book. For example, for courses with the following emphases, the chapters and sections identified below may be of particular interest:

a. The Relationship Between Reading and Writing
   Chapter One: "What Do We Mean By 'Reading'?"
   Chapter Three: "Where to Begin with a Longer Text," "Reading the Hybrid Text," "Reading as Rewriting"
   Chapter Four: "Moving from Poetry to Prose"
   Chapter Six: "Understanding the 'Reading and Writing' Transaction"
b. Literary Genres
   Chapter Two: every section
   Chapter Three: "Reading the Hybrid Text," "Understanding Genre"
   Chapter Four: "Moving from Poetry to Prose"
   Chapter Five: "What You Already Know About Narrative," "How Narrative Can Be Theorized," "Understanding Strange Texts"
   Chapter Six: every section
c. The Importance of Difficulty Across the Curriculum
   Chapter One: "What Do We Mean by Difficulty?" "Why Difficulty Merits Attention," "Tools of Teaching and Learning"
   Chapter Two: "Discovering Your Repertoire"
   Chapter Three: "When a Work Seems Long and Boring"
   Chapter Five: "Reading the 'Story' in 'History,'" "Understanding the Language of Prose"
d. Preparation of Graduate Students
   Chapter One: "What Do We Mean by Difficulty?" "What About the 'Easy' Text?" "Three Tools of Teaching and Learning"

Chapter Two: "Discovering Your Repertoire"
Chapter Four: "Surveying the Landscape"
Every Chapter: "Taking Stock"

Questions You Might Have at This Point

By way of bringing this Preface to a close, let us address several questions you may already be thinking about.

1. To whom is this book addressed?

You will find that this book tends to use two pronouns, "we" and "you." The "we" is, of course, the two of us (the authors) and the experiences we have accrued through our professional work, both inside and outside the classroom. The "you" has several referents. At times, it is the individual student or a group of students. At other moments, it is "you" as teacher and your student(s), working together. And sometimes, it is "you," the teacher, who stands behind the student. When we present especially challenging theoretical material, it is that "you" we are using. At such moments, we are imagining "you" and "us" together, in collaboration, working in concert.

2. Is "difficulty" solely a concern of teachers of English Studies, *of teachers who work closely with issues of reading and writing?*

We hope that it is not. In fact, we think it would be reasonable—and desirable—to think of "difficulty" as an experience that ranges across the curriculum, although figured in different **disciplines** in different ways. While this book is written specifically for the teacher of reading and writing in some area of English Studies, you might find it interesting to know that our approach has been adopted by colleagues in several disciplines.

3. What does a "difficult" classroom look like or sound like?

In a classroom where difficulty is examined, a great deal of conversation is generated, though not necessarily at first. After expressing their confusion, students tend to retreat into a predictable silence. It is at that point that the teacher needs to perform a new kind of move, by posing a different kind of question: What is confusing? Show us. Where did this text surprise you? What did you expect it to do? Where did it fail to meet your expectations? Where did you stop reading? What might be necessary for you to do to resume your reading? What students say in response to these questions is then used to guide classroom inquiry, as they engage in the work of naming what they know and do not know.

If we have not yet made it clear why we have become advocates of teaching *The Elements (and Pleasures) of Difficulty,* let us end with this comment: Our excitement derives from the opportunities it affords us a *teachers.* As teachers, it helps us demonstrate to our students the value of what they already know. It helps us teach our students to teach themselves. And it enables our students to teach us how to encourage their development as learners.

Acknowledgments

First and foremost, we want to thank all our students who, in the classroom and without, keep us hooked on teaching. This book is our tribute to them. Special thanks to the students featured in this book—Sally Amen, Nick Baldwin, Heather Bastian, Patrick Beh-Forrest, Julian Christopher Betkowski, Tom Brennan, Kevin Chysna, Susan R. Connelly, Brendan Cotter, Elizabeth Darcy, Tim Fargus, Liza M. Funkhouser, Emily Ginsberg, Natasha Heard, Nicholas P. Jacobs, Casey Lyons, Michael Mastroianni, Matt Parrott, Kristin Pontoski, Nangula Shejvali, Brand Siegel, Katie Stamm, Eileen Tehan, Kimberly S. Woomer, Erin Wyble, and Trisha Zeytoonjian, for their graciousness in letting us cite their work, for their efforts, patience, and cooperation, for what they let us learn about teaching and learning.

This is a project that has being going on for years, but it has been ignited into completion by a fortunate professional rapprochement with William Covino and by the Carnegie Foundation for the Advancement of Teaching and Learning, which provided such a fertile interdisciplinary ground for the inquiry of difficulty as a learning tool. We are very grateful.

Marilyn De Mario, Bianca Falbo, Jack Hart, and Paul Kameen read early and late drafts of this book. Their insightful suggestions and intellectual support stoked our determination to bring this project to completion. Thanks to the following reviewers for their astute and generous comments, most of which we felt the need to incorporate: David Bartholomae, University of Pittsburgh; David Blakesley, Purdue University; Ann Dobyns, University of Denver; Patricia Harkin, University of Illinois at Chicago; and Hephzibah Roskelly, University of North Carolina at Greensboro. Thanks to William Covino for his elegant editorial guidance, and to Eben Ludlow at Longman for his confidence in this project.

Mariolina Rizzi Salvatori owes a debt of gratitude to Ann E. Berthoff, *primum mobile* of her thinking about reading, writing, teaching and learning; to Patricia Donahue, for her inspiring collaboration; to all her colleagues at the University of Pittsburgh who in their intellectual curiosity have seen possibilities in work that may not fit the usual categories—especially to Dave Bartholomae, Jean Ferguson Carr, Steve Carr, Nick Coles, Joseph Harris, Kathryn Flannery, Lorraine Higgins, Nancy Glazener, Paul Kameen, Margaret Marshall, Shalini Puri, Jim Seitz, and Phil Smith. Thanks to Judith Goleman and Marjorie Roemer for making her believe that this work is worth doing; and to graduate students, past and present, who shared with her the outcome of their own explorations of difficulty.

Patricia Donahue owes (more than) a debt of gratitude to Mariolina Rizzi Salvatori for two decades of intellectual exchange; and to her friends and colleagues at Lafayette College, past and present—especially Bianca Falbo, Bill Carpenter, David Johnson, Robin Rinehart, Monette Tiernan, Bryan Washington, and Suzanne Westfall—who have encouraged and cajoled, teased and tested, advised and soothed. They make an academic life worth living. Lafayette College provided greatly appreciated support in the form of a sabbatical leave. Her years at UCLA introduced her to Ellen Quandahl and Mike Rose, whose influence is evident in these pages. A special thanks to Richard Regosin of the University of California, Irvine, who lit a flame many years ago. And to Joseph Donahue, her first and best reader.

Mariolina Rizzi Salvatori
Patricia Donahue

Preface for Students

> Five or six friends meeting at my chamber, and discoursing on a subject very remote from this, found themselves quickly at a stand, by the difficulties that arose on every side. After we had a while puzzled ourselves, without coming any nearer a resolution of those doubts which perplexed us, it came into my thoughts that we took a wrong course; and that, before we set ourselves upon enquiries of that nature, it was necessary to examine our own abilities and see what objects our understanding were or were not fitted to deal with.

The quotation above is an excerpt from John Locke's preface to *An Essay Concerning Human Understanding,* which he wrote in 1690. Once you come to terms with the strangeness of its language (it is from another place and time), it may be possible to imagine yourself in a similar situation.

Can you remember an experience when a conversation came to a halt—in a classroom or with friends in a favorite meeting place? Maybe you were discussing an abstract concept like "individuality" or the significance of a literary work, or debating the message of a recent movie or DVD. Do you know what made the conversation stall? Perhaps one of you used an unclear word? Or made a claim that unraveled when examined by others? Maybe somebody rebutted a point with an unexpected question?

Locke's response is different. He takes the process of questioning a step further by trying to figure out exactly *why* the conversation stopped. Having noted "the difficulties that arose on every side," he concludes that he and his friends "took a wrong course." He does not say what they did wrong, but one can infer what they did not do. They did not *look at,* they did not account for, they did not examine the difficulties each of them was having. More importantly, they did not consider whether and why *their understandings were or were not fitted to deal with* them.

Locke implies the need for both *pushing the question* and being *self-reflexive*—for *thinking about thinking* itself. And he suggests that an important element of such intellectual work is a confrontation with difficulty: asking questions about what causes it, what it includes, what it reveals about thinking, reading, conversing. By the way, Locke's book, *An Essay Concerning Human Understanding,* developed out of the breakdown in understanding caused by the initial moment of difficulty discussed above. The book has established a long and valued tradition of inquiry both in the humanities and sciences.

Learning from Our Students

Here is an example of a time when one of us (a long time ago!) failed at first to understand why the conversation in her classroom stopped.

The incident happened in an introductory literature course. The text being discussed was Shakespeare's *King Lear*. Several students said they were bored by the play. Others expressed their annoyance with its "old English" kind of language, its elderly and weird characters, its irrelevance. Trying to engage her students in conversation, the teacher asked them to identify places in the text that could account for their responses. One student vehemently complained that Shakespeare unnecessarily complicated the story of *King Lear*. When he was asked to be more precise, he mentioned the two intersecting plots and the similarity in name of two major characters (Edgar/Edmund).

Although he formulated these comments as complaints, the teacher realized that he had in fact noticed two significant features of the play. So, with the best of intentions, assuming the reason for her move would immediately make sense to her student, she read out of a collection of critical essays the following assessment of Shakespeare's technique by literary critic Una-Ellis Fermor:

> Each aspect of technique, then, plays its part in revealing the dramatist's apprehension of life, but plot may fitly follow character here since they merge naturally into each other through the continuous interplay between individual character and even within a

> given play. Plot, indeed, whether simple or complex, single or multiple, may be said to have two aspects, the spatial, which is concerned with character-grouping, and the temporal, which has regard to the order and relation of events ("Character Grouping and Plot," 77–78).

Of course, offered without any suggestion or help as to how to read it or what to do with it, the example did not help the student. Actually, it annoyed him even more. But that moment—a moment the teacher turned over in her mind many times to understand what "she did not do"—was an important one for her. It helped her shape an approach to teaching that capitalizes on the incipient understanding a reader's difficulties may mark.

In a sense, this book is a belated apology to that student. It is an attempt to map out the work that teacher did not know how to do at that time—work that could have prevented her from replacing her student's attempt to understand with conclusions reached by someone else (a "great" critic). It is an attempt to teach students like yourself to trust that when they experience difficulties, there might be good reasons for it. And it is a celebration of what students, when they are listened to carefully, can teach their teachers about teaching.

The Purpose of This Book

The purpose of this book is to help you inquire into whatever intellectual difficulties you might encounter in your work as a college student. Inquiry into difficulty is an important dimension of both academic work and human understanding—a fact that our students' writing has confirmed over and over again. In this book, for practical reasons, we will limit our discussion to some of the most common difficulties readers experience when reading (primarily) literary texts. But the strategies you will acquire for managing these difficulties should help in any course you take.

In a series of seven chapters, focused primarily on different kinds of literary texts—short poems, long poems, short prose, longer prose, the personal essay—this book invites both you and your teachers to undertake a certain kind of intellectual work. That work consists largely of three activities:

- Identifying (and naming) some of the difficulties encountered in reading complex texts
- Examining their nature and effects
- Transforming them into knowledge

In each chapter, you will find a discussion of writing by students much like yourself, produced in response to what we call a "Difficulty Paper Assignment" (another assignment of a different kind is the "Triple-Entry Notebook"). In such a paper, students actually write about their difficulties, try to locate their origin in a particular text, try to figure out how they function and what they mean. In each chapter, you will also be introduced to theoretical terms and concepts, some of which will be placed in **bold** type. Those terms are defined for you in the Glossary at the end of the book. You will also find numerous questions in each chapter ("Reflective Questioning"), designed to bring the knowledge you already possess to light. Each chapter concludes with two sections, "Taking Stock" and "Retrospective": The first offers activities that help you recall or pinpoint what you have learned, and the second presents brief summaries that serve as scaffolds for future work.

Our Assumptions

A textbook that emphasizes difficulties and your ability to identify and make them meaningful is not a typical one. It might interest you to know that as we wrote it, we relied on assumptions we share about students, teachers, learning, and texts. Since we ask you throughout this book to identify your pre-understandings, it seems only fair for us to identify a few of our own. We list some of them below, and others will emerge in subsequent chapters.

- We assume that you already possess a rich repertoire of strategies for dealing with difficulty, but you may not be aware of them. A major purpose of this book is to introduce you to strategies that can foster that kind of self-understanding and self-reliance.
- We assume that this repertoire can be further enhanced through the acquisition of new vocabulary and concepts.
- We assume that you can learn a great deal (as we have) from observing and examining how students like yourself use writing to

name and work through their reading challenges. In virtually every chapter, we rely on student writing to set up certain issues and questions. As teachers, we have found our students' writing about difficulty to be not a revelation of ignorance, but a deeply moving and valuable description of learning.

The Importance of Difficulty

As teachers, we know it is generally not a good idea to put words into our students' mouths or draw conclusions about their feelings. At such moments, students generally react: "Not me!" or "Why would you think that?" And who would blame them? For a brief minute, however, we are going to ignore our own advice and assume that you may be feeling skeptical about our claims. You may be asking "Why is difficulty important?" The answer is that understanding can emerge through an encounter with difficulty, and experiences of reading and writing will be enriched and enhanced if difficulty is addressed rather than ignored. These words may be so counterintuitive as to be unbelievable. Much of education works against this idea. And it is common for students to believe that the best among them are those who make it through with relative ease.

It is our hope that by working with this book in a sustained and careful manner you will be able to answer the question of difficulty's importance for yourself. For now, let us list a few possibilities.

In terms of your work with texts of various kinds, including the literary, an encounter with difficulty will engage you in the true work of the college or the university. Colleges and universities exist, in part, to advance and deepen human knowledge, a process that could not proceed without the recognition of difficulty. In its absence, what would remain is that which is already known, the familiar, the obvious. One of the hallmarks of the culture that colleges and universities nurture and promote is the acknowledgment of difficulty and complexity not as annoyances but fundamental conditions.

A confrontation with difficulty is also important for reasons that extend beyond the academic. For example, what would you say that higher education prepares you for? A job, profession, parenting, adult life, the future, the unknown? Each of these situations is one that promises its fair share of difficult moments. So it is important for you to prepare yourself now, since the habit of confronting difficulty cannot be developed overnight. Think also of the difficulties that take the form of significant social and cultural problems: overpopulation, economic polarization, war, sickness, human suffering of so many kinds. To figure out how to deal with these challenges requires an ability to engage tough questions and design enabling solutions. To make a difference in the world—which is what virtually every student we have worked with has aspired to do—means to face the difficulties of the world.

But we also want to say that an inquiry into difficulty is not only intellectually exciting, it is also pleasurable. That might strike you as a peculiar claim to make (how can hard work be fun?). When you read the work of our students carefully, however, you will notice how often they experience a thrilling epiphany when they locate significance in what had seemed unimportant, confusing, or imponderable. That "aha" reaction, that pride in discovery—such reactions are indications not only of deep learning, but of the deep pleasure that learning can bring.

If difficulty is so important, therefore, why do some students avoid it? We believe that when difficulty is considered a sign of personal deficit or lack, a sign that one has fallen short, students often despair—they feel that they have lost their intellectual compass. They feel their curiosity dissipate. But when difficulty is presented in the positive terms suggested by this book, it becomes a point of departure for a long and satisfying journey of the mind. Students are able to discover how much they already know. They are able to acquire the confidence to explore new terrains, to take intellectual risks. And so we leave you with this idea: The student who is able to articulate, value, and negotiate difficulty will never be at a loss for something to say, something to write about, something to think about. In the world of college and beyond, thinking "with" and "through" difficulty makes a real difference.

Getting Started

This exercise can be done in class, with an assigned partner, or with anybody—a classmate, a relative, a friend—willing to follow the rules. Its function is to make sure the difficulty you are working on "makes sense" to another. That it can indeed be recognized as a difficulty. That the difficulty is "generalizable." That the difficulty can serve as a step toward theorizing the particular interpretive move it requires or makes possible.

And, finally, that it can lead to and sustain the wide and deep investigation of reading required for a final paper.

- Explain to your partner what you found difficult in the text you were reading, and why. Your partner should play back to you what he or she hears you say. If there is mismatch between what is being said and being understood, you should consider how to revise, reframe, and/or clarify the issue.
- Once your partner is satisfied with this initial phase, you can move to the next level of abstraction, the phase in which you begin to articulate the relationship between your difficulty and a possible rule or strategy of interpretation.
- In the next phase, you should assess, in consultation with your partner, whether or not your difficulty can sustain further investigation. Can it become a "project of reading" rich enough to sustain the writing of a research paper, argumentative essay, expository essay? If so, what could that be? Produce an outline, a set of connected questions (if so...then) that might guide your investigation.
- Make your work public in the classroom. Present your project to the class for critique and advice.

It is our hope that repeated practice with this exercise will make it possible for you to internalize the kinds of reflexive moves it maps out for you. You will also notice that you can do this exercise on paper, playing the partner role in your mind.

1

Introducing Difficulty

The difficulty of difficulty is not that it is difficult, but that we do not face difficulty soon enough.

—Hazard Adams, "*The Difficulty of Difficulty*"

Hazard Adams is right. In most educational contexts, learners are not taught to face difficulties soon enough, or at all. One reason may be that the role of difficulties in the learning process is not fully understood; another, that the function of difficulties as elements of understanding is not fully taken advantage of.

In this first chapter, we introduce you to the theoretical understanding about **difficulty** that guides the work of this book. Since we know that the idea of difficulty, especially as a *scaffolding for understanding,* may take some getting used to, we offer you several definitions and consider their theoretical and practical implications. We foreshadow the kind of work we do throughout with student writing, along with the kind of **reading,** writing, and reflecting we will ask you to perform (with considerable guidance from your teachers and the students whose work is featured here).

What Do We Mean by Difficulty?

Based on our work on difficulty with our students, we know that the idea of difficulty as an element of understanding is a challenging one. So we begin with a definition of "difficulty" provided in the most comprehensive dictionary in our language, *The Oxford English Dictionary* (available from your college library in book form or on-line):

> **Difficulty.** 1. The quality, fact, or condition of being difficult; the character of an action that requires labour and effort; hardness to be accomplished; the opposite of "ease" or "facility." . . . c. The quality of being hard to understand; perplexing character, obscurity. 2. with *a* and *pl.* A particular instance of this quality; that which is difficult. a. A thing hard to do or overcome; a hindrance to action. b. Something hard to understand; a perplexing or obscure point or question.

As this definition suggests, "difficulty" is "the quality of being hard to understand." Thus, when we say to you, "Please identify your reading difficulties," we are actually asking you to take notice of what *you* believe is "hard to understand" in a **text.** It might be "hard to understand" for different reasons—because it is perplexing, obscure, mysterious, remote, strange, unfamiliar, uncomfortable, disconnected, meaningless, confusing, ridiculous, contradictory, hypocritical, inconsistent (these are terms our students have used). In other words, we urge you to take notice of whatever slows down or brings to a halt the physical activity of reading, leaving you mystified, wondering why, what, how.

Another point worth noting in the OED definition is that, although it positions "difficulty" in opposition to "ease" and "facility" as something that might require "labor" and "effort," it does not suggest that difficulties are beyond the reach of someone's understanding. A difficulty may be an obstacle, but it is not an unmovable impediment. As one of our students, Kim Woomer, commented: "I looked up the word 'difficulty' in the dictionary. The dictionary stated that a difficulty was an 'obstacle,' which was not what I expected to see. Obstacles are something that may get in one's way, but in no way can they put a complete stop to a process."

Finally, in the complete OED definition of "difficulty" appears one particular quotation, attributed to J. South, and dating to 1716, that we find especially relevant: "They mistake difficulties for impossibilities." That is what we want to promote, an engagement with difficulties that prevents them from bringing to a halt—from making impossible—the challenging work of reading, writing, and thinking.

Why Difficulty Merits Attention

Let us pose two questions that are likely on your mind: Why should difficulty be valued over ease? Why should readers appreciate complexity over simplicity? The questions are reasonable enough, since we are living in a culture (a culture that has not changed much in this respect for several hundred years) in which "ease" is considered a sign of sophistication, intelligence, and talent. Popular belief holds that a genuinely talented artist just sits down and does it, making beautiful canvases and poems appear, seemingly without effort. Tennis players who, at the peak of their form, hit a serve and return a volley (seemingly) effortlessly, are often called "natural," as if they did not have to work to reach that level. And when it comes to the classroom, the good student is supposed to be one who has no difficulty learning quickly, doing work rapidly, and comprehending everything.

It is not that these stories are inaccurate. But they are deceptive because they fail to acknowledge the difficulties the artist, the athlete, and the student had to face, engage, and work through for them to reach the stage of being able to do things in ways that seem effortless and natural. Nobody, not even a genius, *knows* without having *learned* to know.

But, you might ask, "What is the payoff of working with difficulty?" The answer to that question may seem paradoxical. Readers who engage, rather than avoid, a text's difficulties can deepen their understanding of what they read and how they read. If they move away from those difficulties, or opt for somebody solving them for them, chances are that they will never know the causes of those difficulties, and the means to control them. And insofar as reading involves thinking—thinking the thoughts of another, inhabiting somebody else's mind, temporarily adopting somebody else's argument—learning to read in ways that nurture this flexibility of mind can be good preparation for encountering and working through difficult life situations. But, and we want to be clear about this, the process of acquiring this understanding and transferring it to other contexts is not automatic, nor is it simply the result of good will. This is one of the points that come clearly across in the excerpt by Kim Woomer on the next page. Woomer is writing about the difficulty of thinking about difficulty:

I believe the word "difficulty" is very deceiving when one thinks about its meaning. I had always assumed that when one had difficulty with something it means that something is impossible, basically because the task is too complicated for that particular person.

When I first came into this class I discovered that the main portion of writing assignments was to focus on our personal difficulties with individual poems. The first couple of assignments were comprehensible because we would describe our problem and the professor would help us solve it. Then we were asked to locate difficulties as before, but now we were also asked to solve them.

I was extremely confused as to how we could answer our own questions . . . [That's when Kim consults the dictionary and discovers that a difficulty is an obstacle.] This made me realize that the difficulties I have in understanding poetry can be overcome with some extra work. Through this extra work I personally have discovered certain strategies that help me overcome my obstacles.

As Woomer tells us, by *reframing* her understanding of difficulty and by doing extra work, she made an important discovery: There are strategies she can use to work through her difficulties *on her own*. But how did she get there? She got there when she learned to ask of the difficulty she had described the kind of questions that her teacher had asked in the margins of previous Difficulty Papers. Truth to tell, the teacher had not solved those earlier difficulties for her; she had asked questions of them, and reframed them in such a way that enabled Woomer to solve them through strategies she thought of by herself.

Notice also, that although Woomer's Difficulty Paper was produced in response to her reading of a text, what she says about difficulty—her analysis, her hypotheses, her formulations of how to come to terms with it—could be produced in response to any other difficult task. We would say that the payoff for confronting difficulty could not be more powerfully expressed.

What About the "Easy" Text?

Is it ever possible for a "difficult" text to disguise itself as an "easy" one? Can an "easy" text actually be a "difficult" one? Yes, there are many texts that may at first appear simple to read and understand, texts that may trick readers into thinking they are "easy" when they really are not. Take, for example, a book by Lynda Barry, entitled *One Hundred Demons.* It looks like a comic book, and what could be more simple than that? If you look at one page, you may notice that it consists of words and illustrations, that a title is introduced, that an image is presented of a woman drawing, surrounded by pictures that are evidently creations of her imagination. (You might remember reading as a child *Harold and the Purple Crayon*?)

When one of us recently taught Barry's book in a first-year writing course, the class discussion did not get very far, at least not at first. Perhaps because they had been introduced to comic books as children (Barry's variation, the **graphic novel,** is actually quite sophisticated), students were unable to say much initially. Everything seemed too obvious. In their first papers, students did little more than summarize the book's many stories.

But when they were asked to complicate these first accounts by **reading against the grain,** they paid attention to clues they had initially read over. And the result was a highly perceptive analysis. Commenting on the impact of one image on him, and using his understanding of that image as an interpretive clue, one student wrote: "The demon is rising out of the water. *That must suggest* that Barry is dealing with material that was buried and is just starting to surface"; "That bird by her shoulder? Maybe it *suggests* that she's writing about her 'burdens'"; "I thought that an autobiography just told a story about a life. This life *seems much more complicated* than I thought. There's this strange overlay of the present and the past, and something about suppressed desires, if that is what that picture of a heart means." In their next paper, many students acknowledged and then moved beyond their first reactions: "While some readers may view *One Hundred Demons* as a simple comic book, it is actually a story about the complex relationships between past and present identity"; "While *One Hundred Demons* seems to be just a story about a woman's adolescence, it helps us understand why writing is a therapeutic activity"; "By writing *One Hundred Demons,* Lynda Barry provides a system for confronting forgotten memories."

As students put their difficulties in writing, as they write them out, they give themselves a chance to acknowledge the complexity of reading, which, if not *captured through writing,* would easily slide away. As teachers, we have noticed that as students engage the complexities of their reading, the writing that records that engagement also increases in complexity. This is one of the many ways in which the acts of reading and writing complement and interact with each other.

Another genre of writing that may at first seem easy to read—if not always easy to understand—is that of the **textbook.** The textbook is one of those books that students expect to read just to extract a wealth of useful information about the subject, a set of directions on how to execute specific activities that are foundational to a **discipline** (how to speak another language, how to do an algorithm or a lab test, how to interpret literature). The look of textbooks is deceiving. Clean. Arranged into accessible sections. It suggests that learning is orderly and manageable. Maybe. But think about the decisions that had to be made to arrange information in a particular way. Think about what had to be presented first, rather than later. Think about the argument, the central assumptions that shaped the textbook as a physical object. The body of knowledge a textbook presents is usually the end product of substantial prior inquiry, a "journey to knowledge" that remains hidden from readers. To read a textbook for all that is not visible but is part of its conception becomes, then, a difficult task.

What Do We Mean by "Reading"?

In this book, the term "reading" refers to intellectual work, not the mere mechanical act of scanning a written page. Other words for this kind of reading are *active reading, analytical reading,* and *interpretation.*

To clarify what we mean by the work of reading, let us use another word: **transaction.** Think about the nature of transaction, how a transaction is something that occurs between living beings, how getting and keeping a transaction going is determined by its participants. It is possible to think of reading in these terms, as a transaction between *reader and text,* where both play a role in the construction of meaning, where both are understood as participants in a process that must be initiated and negotiated.

But, then, what are we saying about "text"? The words we just used seem to turn texts into human beings, when they obviously are not. But texts also do not emerge by themselves from primal ooze. They are written by human beings, and they convey their human origins in the device of **voice.** In the essays you write, that voice is the self you are attempting to capture, or project, or imagine. In **lyric poetry,** that voice may be the author's **persona** (literally, a term that means "mask") or that of the author herself. In narrative, it can be the voice of the characters or that of the **narrator** who unfolds the scene. In drama, it is the multiple voices of characters in dialogue.

Whoever or whatever that voice is, it cannot be directly contacted. In being *written,* it has been silenced. But, paradoxically, in being *written* it has also been preserved. And it is the responsibility of readers (or, in the case of performance, the actors) to bring it back to life. This is literally the *creative* aspect of reading.

To hear this voice, readers must look for places in the text where it has left traces. When they think they have identified such traces, they need to ask of them, "Might this be what it is and what it meant? Why has this been said? To what end?" Once readers start asking such questions, they are hooked, they are engaged. However, once a text hooks its readers, it is still those readers' responsibility to keep the conversation going by continually checking the conclusions and inferences they make about the text against what the text itself seems to be saying. Clues they look for are the particular words used, sentence constructions, paragraph arrangements, epigraphs, or quotations, and in some cases, footnotes. Their responsibility is to act on their own behalf and on behalf on *that human being conveyed through voice,* which makes the hearing referred to above a complicated business.

There is no right way to initiate this process and keep it going, no rule of thumb. To try to decide whether it is the text or a reader that initiates the process is, from a transactional point of view, a moot point. Suffice it to say that the first words a reader chooses to *focus on,* which are not necessarily the first words he or she looks at, may initiate the process of understanding. They provide the point of entry into a conversation that for somebody else might begin (and end) differently. While a reader can begin almost anywhere, a rich understanding of a text often begins not with what is transparently clear, but with what is perceived (at least at first) as difficult. So, when you encounter moments in a text that seem strange, unanticipated, unpredictable, surprising, or counterintuitive—that is a promising place to begin. *Trust that response.* Consider your uncertainty as a signal for work to be done.

Our students have often asked us where these difficulties are actually located. Do they reside in the text or the reader? (As we said earlier, texts can be perceived to be inert and silent until a responsive reader reactivates the life their authors imagined for them.) We usually answer that difficulties can be thought to exist in both. That is, just as a text's meaning derives from, originates in, a transaction, so do its difficulties. And different readers do indeed name and take note of different difficulties, because these readers possess different personal and academic backgrounds, different repertoires, that make them notice as "unfamiliar" different features of a text. It also occurs, however, that communities of readers (what the literary theorist, Stanley Fish, calls **interpretive communities**) learn to read in similar ways, to value certain textual elements and to disregard others.

How This Book Is Organized

This book consists of seven chapters. Each chapter follows the same format.

- It begins with examples of students' difficulties and with selected aspects of a particular kind of text. This may be a text of a certain length (long or short); a text to which you may bring few or many expectations (as is the case with Shakespeare's plays); or a text representing certain aspects of a type of **discourse** (prose, for example) or a literary **genre** (such as poetry).
- It examines the learning potential of these difficulties, much as Locke proposed in our opening epigraph, by demonstrating how student readers are able to remember a prior and analogous occasion, identify a strategy, and reapply it.
- It concludes with two sections. The first is Taking Stock, which consists of questions, excerpts, and exercises designed to help you reflect on what you have read and learned. The second is Retrospective, which reviews the chapter's main ideas.

Each chapter also undertakes a particular kind of intellectual work (the kind of work commonly done in **English Studies,** and other fields as well), consisting of the following (recursive) stages:

- Initiating the reading process
- Articulating moments of difficulty

- Suggesting how these moments are produced by a body of cultural assumptions about difficulty and understanding, and their place in the development of learning
- Demonstrating the advantages of reflecting on these moments for both students and teachers
- Showing possible connections between students' definitions of difficulty and their assumptions about literature or understanding
- Providing ways to record in writing these moments of difficulty, so they can become visible and release their possibilities

Three Tools of Teaching and Learning

This chapter concludes with three tools that have played a critical role in the development of this project by serving as the stimulus for powerful writing by our students. The first two are the *Difficulty Paper* (conceived by Mariolina Salvatori and adapted by others) and *The Triple-Entry Notebook*. The third is *Reflective Questioning*.

The Difficulty Paper

The assignment for this paper reads as follows. In other chapters of the book, we will present different versions of it.

> You can expect to write regularly in this course. *In preparation for class discussion and writing assignments,* you will write short (1/2 to 1 page) "difficulty papers": these are papers in which you identify and begin to hypothesize the reasons for any possible difficulty you might be experiencing as you read a _______ (a poem, play, essay). Each week, you will write a difficulty paper on one or more of the assigned texts. Each week, I will select one or two of them as unusual or representative examples of the readings you produce. I will photocopy, distribute, and use them to ground our discussions. My goal, in doing so, is to move all of us from judging a difficulty as a reader's inability to understand a text to discerning in that difficulty a reader's incipient awareness of the particular "demands" imposed by the language/structure/style/content of a text.

As the phrase in italics states, this assignment is propedeutic because it helps students *prepare* for class discussion and writing assignments. Responses to this paper are not graded because this work is considered exploratory. The Difficulty Paper can serve at least three purposes:

- It can help students begin to reflect on how they read, and why, and on the kind of understanding their ways of reading can produce.
- It can help students shape a position from which to speak in class and to engage the thoughts of others.
- It can help students to **foreground,** to begin to analyze, and to assess the intricate moves they must make as readers who transact and negotiate with a text.

It is a *difficult* assignment. Interestingly, it is the students who think of themselves as poor, unimaginative readers who view the assignment and its instructions as a validation of the difficulties they experience as they read, and who most insightfully, and readily, turn their moments of difficulty into moments of understanding. But those who think of reading as a relatively uncomplicated process of reception, or a tricky but easily mastered hunt for answers, may think the assignment is trying to peg them at a remedial level to which they do not belong. Some argue that it is not possible to identify, name, and describe a difficulty while experiencing it. If it is difficult, they say, how can we describe it? Others suggest that once it is identified, named, and described, it ceases to be a difficulty. So, what is the use of doing the work the assignment asks of them? And occasionally there are students, usually students who think of themselves as seldom or never having difficulties, and certainly not with reading, who claim that as hard as they try they cannot think of any difficulty they had reading the assigned text.

Over the years, we have learned to mine all of these responses. One of the productive moves such responses have taught us to make has been to enlist the collaboration of students who deny having difficulties in helping those classmates who admit experiencing difficulties while reading a text. In their role as "teachers," these students are asked not to provide answers or interpretations, but rather to give a detailed description of the mental *moves* that might have enabled them to come up with those answers, to construct those interpretations. After a few tries, they admit to finding this practice difficult, since they have seldom or never before been asked to reflect on their own thinking. Thus, they begin to see the complexity of what seemed easy at first and to turn their difficulty into a source of understanding. And real, exciting, collective inquiry begins.

The Triple-Entry Notebook

The Triple-Entry Notebook is a variation of the Double-Entry Notebook, a strategy divulged by a noted theorist of composition, Ann E. Berthoff. Berthoff borrowed and adapted this strategy from the field of science. The strategy allows for identification and isolation of data that are subsequently gathered, grouped, and reflected upon. The Triple-Entry Notebook adds one more stage: the stage in which a reader, having recorded and reflected on what she noticed, tries to come to a conclusion about what the two stages have made possible, and move beyond them. This third stage could be a moment of *resolution* and *self-instruction:* "The difficulty I encountered was due to a set of inappropriate expectations; hence, when reading a text of this kind, I might have to remind myself that . . . " Or it could be the *theorization* of a difficulty that his or her educational assumptions or personal proclivities generate when reading a text of a particular kind. Or it could be the *recognition* of a particular strategy, or convention, used by a writer to work within and against the limits imposed by a genre; in other words, the recognition of an intentional production of difficulty to create understanding.

The addition of a third phase to Berthoff's Double-Entry Notebook is our attempt to reproduce the three phases of understanding that, according to German philosopher (hermeneuticist) Hans-Georg Gadamer, reading can produce. Gadamer names them *erkennen* (to know, to notice something), which the exercise places in the first column; *wiedererkennen* (literally, to know again, to reflect on what one knows or has noticed) in the second column; and *herauserkennen* (to apply, to extend to another context, to raise to another level of abstraction (meta-cognition) what one has learned by reflecting on what and how one knows) in the third column. In the third column, students often produce instances of what educational theorists call **deep learning,** a learning produced through reflexivity and which produces more learning when it is generalized or allied to a new context.

We will provide an example of a Triple-Entry Notebook on the poem "The Business," by the contemporary poet Robert Creeley.

The Business

To be in love is like going outside to see what kind of day

it is. Do not
mistake me. If you love

her how prove she
loves also, except that it

occurs, a remote chance on
which you stake

yourself? But barter for
the Indian was a means of sustenance.

There are records.

Triple-Entry Notebook: "The Business"

Nick Jacobs

Impressions

The theme seems to be suggested in the first line of the poem. "To be in love."

The final thought changes from the original theme, not pursuing the same path as it once did.

Lines are broken (sentences), affecting the meaning of the poem. "If you love" ending the line without specifics.

Questions

How should we utilize the convention of this title?

How should I treat the function of the final line?

"Except that (what) occurs?"

What correlation can be drawn between love and bartering?

Is the final line an extension of the title?

Resolutions

a. Forget about the title for a minute.
b. Forget about the convention of the title.
c. Consider the poem an opposite of the title.

(Bachelard)—the theme of this poem is a house, each new thought is in a different room.

Final line seems to tie everything together.

Impressions	*Questions*
Barter is necessary for life. Love is necessary for life. Love is always a mystery.	How can the rhythm of this piece be determined? Is that determined strictly by using the form of the poem, or can other methods be used?
The line form of the poem seems to function as the punctuation, enabling the poem to be read with a certain rhythm.	Does the final section mean that barter was a way of sustenance for the Indians, just as love is a way of sustenance for the white man?

Reflective Questioning

Throughout this book you will encounter questions interspersed throughout the text. For example, before or after we present a piece of student writing, we might ask questions such as the following, in reference to Nick Jacobs' work:

- What do you think the Triple-Entry Notebook strategy makes visible?
- What does it allow Nick Jacobs to accomplish?
- If the three categories Jacobs has devised do not work for you, which other three categories would you want? Name them.
- What does Jacobs know about poetry that leads him to ask the questions he does?
- What do you make of the last question in the second column?
- How does it follow from the work that precedes and surrounds it?

These questions are not meant to be prompts for writing assignments, although your teacher may want to employ them in that way. We do encourage you to respond to these questions in the form of a journal or class notes, and also use them as topics for class or group conversation. Do not feel obligated to answer every question, or to respond to the questions in a particular order. It may often be the case that the questions you find most *difficult* or *confusing* will be those that generate the most interesting material. Consider these questions as opportunities to make visible the understanding you already possess and to reflect on the kind of work you are learning or need to learn to do.

Taking Stock

Before we move to the next chapter, we invite you to undertake the following tasks:

- Make an inventory of new terms, concepts, and ideas (we will ask you to do this several times throughout the book).
- Design a Triple-Entry Notebook and transcribe terms from your inventory that you think will sustain prolonged inquiry.
- Write a profile of yourself as a reader, writer, and thinker. A useful format might be what is called a **literacy narrative,** a chronology of your experiences with language and your efforts to learn to read and write. What were the first books you read, or were read to you? What was your response? When did you learn to read in school? How did you learn? What kinds of books did you like or dislike to read? When did you learn to write? How? Can you recall any special method of learning? What came easily to you? What was difficult, and why? How would you now characterize yourself as reader/writer/thinker, or some combination of the three? Try to include as many specific scenes of learning as you can.
- Make a list of things you know how to do as a reader: moves that get fruitful results, as well as concepts, strategies, and ideas you have learned as you have worked through this section of the book.

Retrospective

The first chapter—our introduction—aims at preparing you for the work you will do in the following chapters by touching upon issues of definition, format, and practice. It defines difficulty as a moment of confusion that derails the reading process. It places *difficulty* in opposition with *ease,* suggesting that most students have been taught to prefer the latter over the former, and also explaining how certain kinds of texts present a false impression of ease that a careful reading can help to displace. This chapter also introduces you to the nature and format of this book, and provides a rationale for the careful attention it pays throughout to student writing as serious intellectual work. Since reading is a major emphasis of this entire book, it offers a theory of reading (and also of understanding) adapted from Hans-Georg Gadamer. It presents three Tools of Learning. And it surveys some of the reactions students typically have to the study of difficulty.

2

The Difficulty of Poetry

> I came to college dreading the thought of reading another poem. I do not like it when it takes me more than three readings to get the main idea of a poem . . . When a poem does not appear to have a point, or to serve a purpose, I am upset . . . But I like when a poem challenges me enough to make me consider changing a belief that I hold. I like a poem that makes me think.
>
> It's not that I don't like poetry. It's just that it doesn't make sense to me. I have been told over and over again that everyone gets something different from reading the same poem, that even if I don't understand it, I really do. Just in a different way. But it just seems like I'm missing the main point that the poet is trying to put across.
>
> Poetry was not popular among students and teachers at my high school. The students at my high school do not like poetry for some of the same reasons that I do not like poetry . . . I was not taught how to read poetry, the different forms of poetry, or how to analyze poetry. I do not know if the meaning I get from the poem is the right one.

As our three **epigraphs** acknowledge (they lack attribution because they are compiled responses), **poetry** is a particularly difficult genre for many students to read. You may not know where to begin or what you are expected to *get out* of it. It seems to use words in curious ways. Its meaning seems to be *hidden,* neither obvious nor on the surface; it must be *dug out* (think about these **metaphors**). And once the meaning is revealed, it may seem to have little, if any, relationship to the actual words of the poem.

It is precisely because poetry seems so removed from ordinary language, so mysterious and opaque (at least at first), that we begin with it. Most references to poetry in the culture at large undoubtedly propagate the myth of poetry's "strangeness," so there are plausible reasons to wonder where a poem's themes came from. However, it is possible to perform a *successful* reading of a poem (a reading that jolts you into recognition, that enables you to hear yourself thinking in a new and intimate way) by drawing upon the knowledge about words you already possess. As the poet Theodore Roethke reminds us (he was not only a wonderful poet but an informed teacher of poets, and of poetry): "The most difficult thing to remember: that a poem is made of words" (*On Poetry and Craft,* 120).

To be able to read poetry in ways that produce a "jolt of recognition," you must be willing to undertake a demanding form of intellectual work and to keep at it. Understanding does not just happen. But the work it requires has its recompense. As one of the epigraphs cited earlier says: "But I like when a poem challenges me enough to make me consider changing a belief that I hold. I like a poem that makes me think." If a poem is to affect how you think (and feel), you must be willing to confront its obstacles rather than ignore them or gloss over them. For readers who are willing to engage a poem in this way, a special kind of pleasure awaits. It is the pleasure of saying, "this was a particularly difficult text, but I made sense of it on my own, relying on something I already knew and figured out how to apply in a new way." It is the pleasure of poetry itself.

Discovering Your Repertoire

In this book, we recognize and rely on the fact that as readers and students you have acquired a wealth of personal and academic experiences, assumptions about reading, texts, and the so-called world that come into play, consciously or unconsciously, intentionally or automatically, whenever you engage in interpretive acts. This system is your **repertoire.**

Before we examine a particular poem, we ask you to bring to light components of your poetic repertoire, your prior assumptions and experiences with poetry. Consider the questions listed below as a spur to self-understanding. Emend them, or contribute your own. (You may be interested to know that the word "question" comes from the Latin *quaerere*, meaning "to ask" or "to seek." A question is thus a *quest* for understanding.) If you do not think you have anything to say, think about what might be a reason for your lack of confidence. While there are no correct answers, not just any answer (particularly "yes" or "no") will do. This exercise is productive only insofar as it conveys accurate, thoughtful, and thorough reflections on your reading processes:

- Provide some examples of poetry. Explain what you think makes them poetry. How do you define "poetry"? If you were to say to a friend, "I'm reading poetry in my English class," how would you make that friend understand what you are doing?
- Would you agree or disagree that poetry is not popular (see third epigraph)? Why do you think that is? Are there forms of poetry that are not immediately recognizable as poetry?
- Try to remember the first poem you ever read. Where? When? What kind of experience was this for you? Write down any particular memories you associate with that early event. Do they come to mind when you read poetry? Do they affect your reading of poetry? How?
- Take stock of what you have been taught about poetry in school. Try to recall any special terms your teachers have used, and any special instructions or recommendations for reading they gave you.
- What have you learned about poetry outside the classroom: from films (*Dead Poet's Society*, for example), other books, friends, social events? How is this knowledge similar to or different from your school knowledge?
- Have you ever written a poem? Did you show it to anyone? What was the response? In what ways is writing a poem different from reading a poem?

As you reflect on the answers you give, think of them as stemming from your repertoire. The repertoire of assumptions, experiences, and ideas you have about poetry will either assist you in reading complex texts or undermine your efforts. If you believe you dislike poetry, for example, you may be unwilling to engage in the process of careful, attentive, and slow reading. If you have ever written a poem, you may think that all poetry is confessional and dominantly personal, an idea that will hinder your efforts to read poetry written before the twentieth century. An important reason why we begin our discussion of poetry by asking you to think about your repertoire (a move we would encourage you to repeat at any point in this book where a new kind of text, genre, discourse is introduced) is that if your repertoire enables you to produce a complex reading, then you need to know why, so you can repeat certain moves with different poems. And if it hinders such a reading, then you need not only to explore how and why, but also to revise it—emend, enlarge, question, suspend certain elements, substitute others. But we want to emphasize that you cannot change what you have not yet recognized and named. Once that work has been done, you can then make a conscious decision to suspend certain kinds of judgments, to refuse to put certain assumptions into play. You can enrich and complicate your repertoire by reading more poetry, by asking strategic questions about what you have read, and by writing about your reading. The sections that follow will help you engage in precisely this kind of work.

Reading "One Art"

Here is a brief and enigmatic poem by Elizabeth Bishop. Once you read it, we are going to ask you to do work with it in several ways: by reflecting on your initial reading process; by rereading the poem and annotating it with a notational system you design alone or in collaboration with your classmates; by sharing your annotated text with others; and by inferring from the pattern of notations the poem's major and marginal emphases and kinds of difficulties it is understood to evoke.

One Art

The art of losing isn't hard to master;
so many things seem filled with the intent
to be lost that their loss is no disaster.

Lose something every day. Accept the fluster
of lost door keys, the hour badly spent.
The art of losing isn't hard to master.

Then practice losing farther, losing faster:
places, and names, and where it was you meant
to travel. None of these will bring disaster.

I lost my mother's watch. And look! my last, or
next-to-last, of three loved houses went.
The art of losing isn't hard to master.

I lost two cities, lovely ones. And, vaster,
some realms I owned, two rivers, a continent.
I miss them, but it wasn't a disaster.

—Even losing you (the joking voice, a gesture
I love) I shan't have lied. It's evident
the art of losing's not too hard to master
though it may look like (*Write* it!) like disaster.

We ask you to begin your work with this poem by thinking about how long it took you to read it. Did you read it once, or several times? Did you stop at any point? Did you read it aloud or silently? If this is a difficult poem, and we think it is, what makes it difficult?

Now reread the poem, this time with pen or pencil in hand in order to mark the text. Employing any **system of notation** that works for you (perhaps you can create a notational system with your classmates), write between the lines of the poem and in its margins. By "notational system," we mean a pattern of marks readers employ to remember certain elements of a text, to record their reactions to it. Such notations function as a method of retrieval, allowing readers to return to a text, recall their first impressions, move beyond, and complicate them. Readers who employ a system of notation find themselves reading more actively, since while they read they think about and write to a text. Sometimes responses take the form solely of direct questions or comments: readers "talk to" the voice. Usually they combine comments and coded symbols, such as the following:

?	question or confusion
→	connects to
___	central idea
!	surprising idea, something unexpected, etc.
[ ]	brackets around similar terms, or confusing words, or repeated terms
( )	circles around words to make them stand out

Using whatever symbols that make sense to you (circles, triangles, squares, asterisks, straight lines, squiggly lines, stars, and so on), mark those places that for any reason you find difficult. It is especially productive to identify those moments where the forward thrust of reading itself came to a stop because you had to go back to reestablish a thread, or you simply did not know what the words were asking you to imagine or to think.

Now photocopy your annotated text for one or two classmates (who will have done the same). Exchange your texts. What do you see? Did any of you mark the same places? Did you seem to read the poem in the same way? Are you surprised by your classmates' notations? You can use the following questions to sharpen your analysis:

- What kinds of marks are used? Ask each reader to explain them.
- Based on what is and is not marked, and how, describe what you think different readers are looking for. Do certain kinds of words recur? Words used in a non-ordinary way? Repetitions (both words and sounds, in the form of rhythm and rhyme)? Punctuation? What about moments of change, disruption, violation of pattern? How closely do the notations of various readers resemble each other?
- Write down which inferences you feel you can make about how each reader read, based on the notations. For example, many marks would suggest engagement rather than passivity. Arrows might suggest an interest in correspondences. Written comments might suggest a desire to talk back.

Reading Elizabeth Bishop: Liza Funkhouser

We now want you to look at a piece of writing on the next page about difficulty generated by a student, in a classroom similar to the one you are in. Liza Funkhouser produced this piece of writing during Week 1 of a composition course (Reading and Writing About/Through Poetry) in response to the Difficulty Paper Assignment provided in the introduction to this book.

In the second to last line of the poem "One Art," Elizabeth Bishop is speaking of how the art of losing isn't hard to master. The line which follows it also goes with the flow of the poem, with one exception. The phrase "(*Write* it!)" is inserted into the middle of the line. (Similar examples can be found in Robert Bly's poems. Take the last line of "Snowfall in the Afternoon," for instance. Why does he mention blind sailors after painting a scene of a farm? Another line that seems oddly placed is in "Driving My Parents Home at Christmas." It is the one concerning the falling oak. Why did Bly elect to place that line where he did, and what is its significance to the poem?) [These poems are provided in the Appendix.]

The first point we want to make about Funkhouser's response is that what she notices about the poem *is indeed worth noticing.* What she perceives as a perplexing moment in the poem is a moment central to the workings of the poem itself. She has not made a "mistake." She is not failing to "get something" because she does not know much about the interpretation of poetry or the technical language used to analyze it. In noticing that a line is oddly placed, she is responding to one of the demands the poem's language and structure make on its readers—to stop, to take notice. She sees something that is central to what the poem, arguably, is trying to do. She sees that something has been inserted into the poem that disrupts what she calls its "flow," and she asks why. She seems to be guided by a logic that makes her puzzle at what she calls "oddly placed" lines. At this point in the course, she asks a good question, but she does not follow through with it.

As you have probably noticed, the flow of Elizabeth Bishop's poem is indeed suddenly interrupted by the persona's admonition (to herself? to the reader?) to write something that seems to have been painstakingly avoided: the acknowledgment that although "the art of losing isn't hard to master," nobody escapes it (Is "it" the process of turning something into an art? Of losing something? Of becoming resigned to losing something?), and "it" may look like disaster. Up to the last line, "disaster" has been named but at the same time denied ("their loss is *no* disaster"; "*None* of these will bring disaster"; "but it *wasn't* a disaster"). The end of the poem seems to want to end the cycle of denial. In fact, this cycle must end because the loss identified in the final lines is one that cannot be mastered—or suppressed—as neatly as the others, or she would not need to "*Write* it!" Her defense mechanisms seem to have broken down.

The insertion of the parenthetical phrase does indeed stop the poem's flow, disrupts it as does the repetition of "like." But that forced stop leads the reader to pay attention to a disruption—and a powerful recognition—that the flow might otherwise smooth over and prevent her from noticing or admitting. What the student, prompted by the assignment, identifies as a difficulty proves to be that part of the poem that the poet is obviously calling attention to. What the student sees as a problem is better understood as a **strategy.**

We can understand this reader's comment on the disruption of flow in another way: as a reaction by a student who has probably been told repeatedly that for writing to be good, it must have "flow." Elizabeth Bishop, a highly respected poet, must know the rules. That makes her violation even more surprising. What is it that the student has missed?

She has not missed anything. In fact, she has noticed something—a disruption. Her attention to this disruption suggests considerable sensitivity to the operations of poetic language, but because she assesses these moves—and her own reaction to them—in terms of prior assumptions about language, she interprets what she has noticed as a sign of misunderstanding rather than of poetic design. In fact, you might be interested to know that her expectation about logic, even if she might have criticized Bishop for her mistake or blamed herself for the moment of disjunction, is one shared by experienced readers of poetry. In *Poems, Poets, Poetry: An Introduction and Anthology*, Helen Vendler, noted poet and literary critic, has this to say about the ordering of language in poetry: "Because poetry is a temporal art, it has to unfold sequentially, one piece after another. First I say x, then y, then z. But the logical relations among x, y and z may not be additive or sequential ones" (152). As Vendler explains, sentences, phrases, words, or sounds may be arranged to emphasize relations of resemblance, they can also be arranged differently, to emphasize relations of contrast and juxtaposition. Look again at "One Art" in terms of its logic or sequencing: Where do you find points of resemblance or similarity? Difference or contrast? Consider how these textual features may function as clues toward interpretation.

If you were to respond to the work done by the student above through Vendler's quotation, what additional work would you say she can do? Imagine, for example, that she were to ask "why" the poem offers this moment of disruption. What possible answers might she give? What other questions might follow from her answers? What are the benefits to her as a reader of asking "why" what she has noticed is important rather than assuming that she has made some kind of mistake?

Here is a different poem, which we ask you to mark as you did before, this time taking into account what Vendler says about logic and sequence. Attempt to identify moments of resemblance and difference within this poem by taking notice not only of the meaning of words and phrases but of their sound and their actual appearance on the page.

Donald Justice, "Hands"

Les mains ne trouvaient plus
De bonheur dans les poches.

—Guillevic

No longer do the hands know
The happiness of pockets.

Sometimes they hang at the sides
Like the dead weights of a clock.

Sometimes they clench into fists
Around the neck of anger.

Formerly they were brothers
To clasp, shoulders to rest on.

If now they unfold like maps,
All their countries seem foreign.

They dream of returning to
The dark home of the pockets.

They want to wash themselves clean
Of the blood of old salutes.

To scrub away the perfumes
Of the flesh they have tasted.

And all that they grasp is air.
Think of the hands as breathing,

Opening, closing. Think of
The emptiness of the hands.

Reading as Participatory: Liza Funkhouser and Kim Woomer

> Reading poetry is an encounter with one's depths. It is a participatory relationship, demanding intimacy with what the poet is asking for—deeper contact with another, deeper contact with oneself.
>
> —Edward Hirsch

We expect Hirsch's description of poetry in his book *How to Read a Poem and Fall in Love with Poetry* (he is himself a poet) to resonate with many readers. But at the same time, we expect that readers who do not feel comfortable with poetry might skeptically question his description. They might point out that the words he uses, a metaphor ("an encounter with one's depths"), beg several questions, and obscure, although gracefully, the intricate work a reader's mind must do so that her depths and the poet's depths come into a participatory relationship. And we would agree.

Yet as Natasha Heard reminds us in one of the epigraphs to this chapter, while there is great satisfaction to be gained from such a participatory relationship, readers "tend to be reluctant" to do the required work. For Heard, they feel this reluctance because they don't know "how to get started." Here is what she says about her own reading process:

> At one time when I would read and didn't understand what a text was saying, I skipped over it like it was not there. After being confronted with challenging material, I see the necessity to penetrate into what is causing me confusion. In poetry a difficult line is sometimes the key to interpreting the entire poem. It is often what makes the poem unique and interesting. The author often purposely adds a difficult line to encourage its readers to take a deeper look into the writing.

Whether poets insert difficult lines to encourage readers to take a deeper look at the writing, or whether a difficult line marks the moment when the poet tries to overcome the inevitable limits of her medium and, in a gesture of trust, submits that "problem" to her reader's interpretation, is something that cannot be easily settled. As you work through *The Elements (and Pleasures) of Difficulty* and learn to understand and address poetry's challenges, you will decide. In the meantime, we want to examine examples of writing that powerfully enact a participatory relationship between reader and poem.

The first response is by Liza Funkhouser, written at week 4 of the course:

> The first two lines of "Hands" by Donald Justice were very intriguing. After reading that first sentence, I was forced to stop and re-read it. Initially, I stopped because I found the sentence to be very dynamic in the sense that it could have many different meanings if just read alone. I then found myself asking why the hands were not happy out of the pockets. I guessed that the rest of the poem would explain my question, so I began to read the poem again from the beginning.
>
> I read the poem through, but could not fit the pieces together all at once. Since the poem was divided into short stanzas, I decided to read each of them one by one. Breaking the poem down in this fashion helped me tremendously.
>
> I took the first stanza as meaning that the hands were no longer sheltered in pockets, but out in the world which at times could be a very happy place. The next stanza implied to me that sometimes the "owner" of the hands did not know what to do or say so his hands just hung by his side. The third stanza also dealt with the owner's feelings. His feelings of anger could be those towards people and/or situations.
>
> The fourth stanza changed the rhythm and flow of the poem by not beginning with the word "sometimes" and by not giving a description of what the hands would do; instead, it described what they *used* to do. The usage of the words "formerly," "brothers," and "shoulders" implied that the owner who was once surrounded by caring and supportive friends and family now finds himself alone.
>
> The next stanza gave me a bit of trouble. I couldn't find a connection by just reading the words. After reading it a few times, I tried "unfolding" my own hands. Doing this gave me the idea that maybe the owner is alone because he is in a strange place his hands don't recognize and that is "foreign" to their owner. If that is the case, then the sixth stanza would mean that not only do his hands want to return to their home (the pockets), but so does their owner want to return to his home.

The next two stanzas, I found, could have two meanings. The first, and more literal, is that the owner is a soldier at battle in a foreign land who wishes to forget the turmoil and death the fighting has caused. The second is not so literal, and is the one which I lean toward. The owner has made some bad friendships, which he would like to forget. He would also like to rid himself of any undesirable affairs ("perfumes/Of the flesh") he may have had.

The owner, in the last stanza, is trying to pull himself back on track, but all he manages to "grasp is air." He tries desperately to clasp something—anything—by opening and closing his hands. He fails, and without anything to hold onto, the owner's life is very, very empty.

This is the response of a reader who has grown considerably over a period of a few weeks, who has acquired confidence in her perceptions, and has learned to view difficulties not as problems but as provocations.

Almost immediately, Funkhouser identifies a problem *in the poem:* the different meanings (**ambiguity**) of the first sentence. Although she had to stop, or possibly because she did stop, she declares *it* "intriguing." She attributes the poem's "dynamic" to its ambiguity, its multiplicity, its possibilities. She asks questions about the poem—"why" are the hands "not happy out of the pockets"?—and trusts that the poem will supply an answer. "Trouble" does not bother her anymore. Her "repertoire" has been enlarged to include terms such as "stanza" and "literal." She has begun to understand poetry, as Vendler recommends, as a temporal process, whose meaning and significance unfold in stages, whose form raises expectations and then either satisfies, defers, or disrupts them (see her comment on the fourth stanza). Her reading is participatory: active and analytical. She performs a kind of intellectual work that enables her to reflect on her reading as she is reading to decide which meanings might be in need of revision. She respects what Molly Peacock refers to as "Our obligation . . . to balance the reality of the poet's vocabulary with the force of the reaction it provokes in us" (143).

Now here is Kim Woomer's response to the same poem prompted by the same Difficulty Paper Assignment. Woomer was Funkhouser's classmate—same teacher, same texts, same classroom.

I was confused by the poem "Hands" by Donald Justice. I understood the words and ideas which the poem was expressing, but I was unclear as to exactly what these ideas were describing.

I believe that Justice wanted to get a deeper relation across than just a relationship to hands. He describes the hands as being "at home" in pockets. Even though the pockets are dark, the hands still wish and dream of returning to them. When the hands are not in the pockets they just hang as if they were unhappy at their present place. The poet also says the hands only experience foreign objects whenever they unfold or reach out. In the last stanza, the poet describes the hands as having complete emptiness as they would move around. By the poet discussing all of these in-depth concepts I definitely believe that he must be describing something more than just a set of hands.

One possibility is that he was using his hands to represent himself and his emotions. He used pockets to symbolize his home where he felt totally comfortable and safe. He must have lost his home somehow because he states that his hands are not near the pockets (home) anymore. I believe he is very uneasy about this new place. He describes the hands as longing to return to the pockets. He also relates hands to emptiness which is what he must be feeling in the absence of his original home.

Using our examination of Funkhouser's writing as a model, examine Woomer's reading process in a similar way. Where does she begin, and why? Where does she move to next, and why? How does Woomer's reading differ from Funkhouser's? Do they notice different things? Do they react to them differently?

When two examinations of the same poem are presented side by side, as we did in the section above, interesting questions may arise. For example, which one is better, stronger, more successful? (Answers to these questions will differ, of course, depending on one's ideas about what a poem should do and what one means by verbal success.) Or, is it possible that one reading cancels out or disproves the other, especially if it is believed that a poem does indeed have a single correct meaning? Finally, for some readers, the juxtaposition of two interpretations will provoke no reaction at all, especially if they believe that "everyone has his or her own opinion."

The issue raised by these considerations is actually quite important: Can a literary text be understood to have several meanings? The answer, quite simply, is "yes." But why? First, let us dismiss the idea that everyone has "his or her own" opinion as not bearing up to scrutiny, for several reasons. Most of our opinions have a source outside ourselves—parents, friends, teachers, books, television, film, history—even if the moment of their acquisition is long forgotten. Furthermore, the range of opinions on any given issue is actually rather small. But what is interesting to us is that the expression of this opinion about opinion is often itself a strategy for ignoring and circumventing difficulty.

Because literature is complex and ambiguous, it can indeed have multiple meanings. It can be said to be **multivocal** or "many voiced." (At this point we expect you to ask questions about our use of language. But we also expect you to start using whatever available resources you have to solve any initial lexical and conceptual difficulty.) One reading of a text may contradict another. But it can also serve to complement or enrich it. Rather than be locked into an either/or position, it might be more productive to inquire into the differences that are the source of disagreement (for example, differences in repertoire; or, to turn the matter on its head, similarities in repertoire). To summarize, we would say that while different readers might construct different interpretations, not every interpretation is equally compelling.

Distinguishing Between Ordinary and Metaphorical Language

Your work in this chapter up to this point has focused on your preexisting ideas about poetry, and how students like yourself can use and did use writing to engage in a reading process that steadily increased in its ability to engage difficulty. Now, we shift from student self-reflection, which in a Triple-Entry Notebook would be in the second column, to theories of poetry and its language by language specialists and literary critics. This is the kind of **metalanguage** that in a Triple-Entry Notebook would be in the third column. This material is presented to enlarge your repertoire, but, more importantly, to demonstrate how closely your work with difficulties resembles that by expert readers and to reaffirm how close you come to do with difficulties what theorists have been trained and have learned to do with them.

When students are asked to name what they consider some of poetry's characteristic elements, they consistently mention "hidden meanings," **"images"** and **"metaphors,"** and "rhythm." What we find intriguing is that these elements are the sources of much of poetry's difficulties. At the same time, without them (and other distinguishing elements) poetry would not be poetry. They account for and make possible poetry's economy, imaginativeness, evocativeness, allusiveness, and at times, meaningful obscurity. And if you look at these features of poetry, you will notice that none of them can be apprehended or understood, immediately and unequivocally. Once again, when students focus on these elements as elements of difficulty they are actually acknowledging poetry's special and specific features.

While students will invoke their lack of experience with poetry as their obstacle to understanding it, they always have some fundamental knowledge of ordinary language that enables them to notice both the deviation of poetic language and its difficulties. But they do not know how to turn what they notice into understanding, or to construct a persuasive interpretation of why they believe it is important and worth noticing. Remember Kim Woomer's response to "Hands"? She begins by saying that while she understands the poem's "words and ideas," she cannot figure out what "these ideas were describing." She then proceeds, in spite of herself, to offer a thoughtful reflection on what "hands" might represent. She knows that the poet "must be describing something more than just a set of hands," but thinks of herself as confused.

Perhaps you need further convincing of your verbal skill? Ask yourself, have you ever grasped for words to convey the power of emotions you felt, or to describe a tangle of complicated and contradictory responses to a situation? Have you, in these cases, ever said, "It was like [whatever]"? If you did (it is impossible for you never to have done it), you resorted to metaphorical language. Actually, to be precise, you used a "simile," a turn of phrase (a figure of speech, a trope) that is introduced by "like" or "as," and in so doing, you called attention (even if you didn't know you were doing it) to the comparison you were making. Metaphors look like **similes** without "like" or "as." The absence of those two little words does something remarkable to how, if we reflect on it, we think through this use of language. That absence turns a comparison into an identity: *like* becomes *is*. Metaphors tend to be more complicated than similes because they activate the transfer of multiple traits. In the metaphor "love is a rose," so much is being intimated (and as a reader, you must do the work of unpacking): Love is natural and lovely, beautiful but dangerous, alive but poised to wilt (a less obvious possibility was provided by a student who said that, like a rose, love can be purchased on the street corner!). But in the simile—her complexion is like a rose—the domain of transference is more narrow. In the case of both metaphor and simile, words are poetic, not because they are inherently different from everyday words (a rose is a rose, after all), but because they have been *used* in a poetic way.

A helpful perspective is provided by Jan Mukařovský, a Czech linguist who examined the difficulty of deciding how to read language as "ordinary" (his word is "standard") or "poetic." He begins by asking: "Is poetic language a special brand of the standard, or is it an independent formation?" (This is a common move in theoretical inquiry, by the way, starting with definitions and delineating differences. It is a move we encourage you to adopt.) And he answers this important question by posing further questions about the features of poetic language and deducing his answer from the observations those questions produce: "Poetic language is thus not a brand of the standard . . . for poetry, the standard language is the background against which is reflected the aesthetically intentional distortion of the linguistic components of the work, in other words, the intentional violation of the norm of the standard" (42). He adds: "The function of poetic language consists in the maximum of foregrounding of the utterance . . . In poetic language foregrounding achieves maximum intensity to the extent of pushing communication into the background . . . it is not used in the service of communication, but in order to place in the foreground the act of expression, the act of speech itself" (44–45).

What have we learned from this discussion? While the words used in ordinary and poetic language may be the same (after all, look at the poems we have included in this chapter; did they contain any words you did not know?), their function changes with a shift in **context.** In ordinary language, whose function is unimpeded communication (thus the importance placed on clarity), words recede so as to enable content to step forward (to be foregrounded). In poetic language, however, a poem draws attention to its own "poem-ness," identifies itself as belonging to the genre of poetry, foregrounds the nature of the **utterance** itself, and thus invites a particular kind of reading—reading for ambiguity and complexity.

To cast an eye on our own sentences, we spoke of content as *stepping forward*—using a device called **personification,** whereby intangible qualities are assigned human characteristics. If this language occurred in a poem, something might be done to make you linger on it, some shift in line or pacing perhaps; here, however, our goal in using this personification is clarity—to help you understand a difficult concept more easily.

Moving Beyond the Literal: Katie Stamm

Mukařovský's essay was one assigned in this course on poetry. Let's take a look at Katie Stamm's response to it:

> It appears from this essay that the reason we often have difficulty with *a poem is because of poetry's "foregrounding," which is the process* of consciously performing an act . . . By pushing the act of communication into the background, so that expression can be foregrounded, poetry *inhibits itself from being understood.* Communication is a link between the reader and the writer. If communication is pushed into a secondary position, then it becomes harder to get the message across. Expression is important, but if communication is absent, I do not believe that expression can complete its job on its own. We can express ourselves but if communication is not as important, then we cannot receive response to what is being expressed.

As Stamm notices, the language in poetry draws attention to itself in ways that "ordinary" language—language whose purpose is communication—does not. The difficulties one encounters when reading poetry are central to its nature as a genre, as a type of literature: Poetry uses language in ways that rub against and inhibit everyday communication in order to help us see things in new ways. There is a group of theorists called the Russian Formalists who say of poetry that it **defamiliarizes**—it restores mystery to what is taken for granted, makes the stone "stoney," restores freshness to our perceptions, by calling upon us to look more carefully. Stamm's comments resonate with Edward Hirsch's when he says: "The transaction between the poet and the reader, those two instances of one reality, depends upon **figurative language**—figures of speech, figures of thought. Poetry evokes a language that moves beyond the literal and, consequently, a mode of thinking that moves beyond the literal" (13–15).

Once again, it is a matter of the reader being willing to undertake a particular kind of work. The critic Donald Davidson explains that "understanding a metaphor is as much a creative endeavor as making a metaphor, and as little guided by rules" (*On Metaphor*, 29). Take for example a metaphoric use of language, such as "her words ooze hostility." What are we to do with it? Katie Stamm helps us proceed:

> Take note of the metaphors or images that are being produced. This is a technique which was introduced to me by Brooks and Warren. Through the identification of metaphors the reader can begin to identify a characteristic of the poem's language, which is very important. If the reader can identify a metaphor, then she is able to realize that the poem is speaking figuratively or semiotically, and the reader will be able to translate the text into familiar terms.

And she provides an example:

> This whole stanza ("The Abortion") needs to be looked at closely . . . I had to look closely at the lines: "the grass as bristly and stout as chives, and me wondering . . . " (Sexton, 505). She wanted the reader to form a visual picture as well as recognize that she could not handle the pain she was feeling. She wants the reader to imagine that this blade of grass is far stronger than herself, but we're only able to do this after we realize that the words are not to be taken literally. It is rewarding to see the tremendous improvement I have made from the first difficulty paper up to the final assignment.

What can we learn from Stamm's work? That first, as readers, we must recognize that words are being used metaphorically. Then we can undertake the work of translation.

At this point, we ask that you read Stamm's writing, doing the kind of notational work you did earlier. Trace the reading and thinking moves she makes and reflect on the writing they produce. Mark, in fact, specific words and turns of phrase that seem to flag moments of doubt, reflection, and resolution. Again, it is a matter of the reader doing the work, of being creative, of not settling for the quick and easy response.

Taking Stock

At the end of Chapter 1, we asked you to make an inventory of new terms, concepts, ideas. Take a look at that list. If you understand those terms—or some of them—differently, and you must have if you have engaged this process of learning, how would you describe that change? What has caused it?

- Which of the terms you entered in your Triple-Entry Notebook is getting more attention from you? Why? Which of the columns is easier or more difficult to write in? Which is the most crowded?
- What has changed in the moves you make as a reader, writer, and thinker?
- Having worked through this chapter, how might you revise your literacy narrative? What, now, could you include in it?
- Write two paragraphs of instruction and advice to a student who is now beginning the journey of learning you began at the beginning of the course. What would you want him or her to know? What did we not take into account that we could have? (We promise to include the most fruitful suggestions by students in our future revision of this textbook.)

Retrospective

This chapter put into practice several of the ideas introduced in the previous one. It focused on poetry, a genre more familiar than you know. To enable you to excavate your preunderstandings, it introduced the idea of "repertoire" and asked you to reflect on your assumptions and experiences. Through a close reading of several student texts, this chapter then demonstrated how a repertoire can operate either as a passageway or a dead end. It asked you to develop a system of notation in order to create a visual record of your reading process and a retrieval system for additional work. Finally, it introduced several ideas about language—in particular, the difference between "ordinary" and "metaphorical" language.

3

The Difficulty of Longer Texts

> I notice a lot of repetition of words, phrases, and ideas. I wonder if there is a pattern or special significance to these repetitions.
>
> —Kristin Pontoski

> The process of asking questions about a particular text forces me to read very closely and consider all the text's elements. As a result I found myself answering my own questions and drawing my own conclusions.
>
> —Eileen Tehan

In Chapter 2, we asked you to make visible your pre-existing knowledge about poetry so you could reflect and build on it. Our intention was to suggest that knowledge you have acquired over the years in school and through informal encounters with public poetry in the form of advertisements, web sites, billboards, greeting cards, e-mail, television, computer games, and rap music is knowledge that you can adapt and transfer to different kinds of texts. But how does this transfer happen? What rules guide it?

We wish we could provide such rules. But the fact is that the process of reading is so complicated that it cannot be reduced to a set of procedures. No specific rules can be offered for how and when to transfer what one understands in one context to another. What we can say, however, is that when readers confront new versions of an idea—or issue, category, or text—they tend to formulate the new in terms that they already know, in terms that are already a part of their repertoire. This is a form of transfer, and it is a fundamental principle of knowledge formation.

However, sometimes the transfer is productive; sometimes it is not. When there is a "mismatch" between new ideas and the old frameworks used for making sense of them, readers tend to experience difficulty, confusion, a "say what?" moment. For example, consider the highly successful advertising campaign by Apple Computers Inc., presenting a picture of a person admired for his or her inventiveness, quirkiness, brilliance—such as Albert Einstein—and including the caption, "Think Different." A reader who reads the ad from the perspective of grammatical correctness might decide that the words are wrong, that they make no sense. Indeed, "different" should actually be "differently." It is an adverb. Its grammatical function is to modify the verb. However, to read this caption in terms of literal accuracy blocks the understanding the caption seems to want to generate. Let us suppose a reader approaches the ad differently. Rather than label it as incorrect and be done with it, let us assume that reader asks: What does to "Think Different" mean? Did the ad's designer actually mean "differently"? Or is it asking that in recognizing Einstein we immediately associate "different," as the quality of being different, with him and with the product that is being advertised? Consider this. Stumbling on the meaning of "different," noticing and thinking through its ambiguity, makes us invest it with alternative meanings. This would not happen if we dismissed the caption because it *is* grammatically incorrect, or if we did not notice that one way of reading it *makes it* grammatically incorrect.

A reader who uncovers the difficulty of the caption makes the words "Think Different" become rich in possibilities. She transfers to the ad her understanding of poetic language and the possibility of multiple and simultaneous meanings. She understands that the caption's kind of ambiguity—its play between what is said and what is not said—is similar to that typical of poetic language, and that like poetic language it calls for a reader's mental agility, which it rewards with the pleasure of special accomplishment. The language of the ad invites us to "Read (what is) Different": that is, to read following pre-established tracks, *while* being attentive to when they might lead us down well-trodden paths; or following them *while* reflecting on the steps being taken; or following them *and* reflecting on the different pathways to understanding they might cut off.

So, what kind of different reading are we asking you to perform? In the previous chapter on reading poetry, we explored the matter of what a "different reading" (or reading differently) might be with reference to short lyric poems (compact, rhythmic, emotionally intense) written during the past 20 years. Those poems were certainly difficult. But their brevity allowed for repeated, intense readings, which rekindled and kept prior (if competing) meanings present in your mind as you formulated new ones. In this chapter, we are going to look at a different kind of text and a different set of difficulties. The text is *The Rime of the Ancyent Marinere,* a long poetic composition written by Samuel Taylor Coleridge in the early nineteenth century. Your teacher may have provided you with a copy, or you may have purchased one. Since this poem is in what is called the "public domain," it is readily available on the Internet. You may want to use the following site (as you will discover or your teacher will tell you, Coleridge revised this poem throughout his life, so different versions are available): http://etext.lib.virginia.edu/stc/Coleridge/poems/Rime_Ancient_Mariner.html. We will ask you to reflect on the processes of understanding you use as you work through this text. As you draw on your prior experience reading short poems, consider how the time it takes to read and re-read this text affects your grasp of it. You will need to use different reading strategies. Your processes of understanding will work differently. Consider also how writing—notes, marginal comments, a journal, a Difficulty Paper—might help you temporarily capture, to later retrace, the meanings you compose and might forget as you move along.

As usual, we ask you to begin this exploration by doing some written work. Think about longer poems you might have read and the kinds of reading difficulties you encountered in reading them. If you stopped reading the text at any point (do you remember where?), what made you stop? What prevented you from pushing ahead? How would you define the challenges that longer poems pose? (You may want to review your list of difficulties from Chapter 2.) Would you characterize those differences as ones of quantity or quality or both?

When a Work Seems Long and Boring

We are going to make a different kind of move at this point. We will try to anticipate your first reaction to the poem, based on how many of our students have *initially* responded to it over the years. Like them, you may have said it is boring. You may have made that claim, in fact, even before you read it, based on its length, its division into stanzas, its odd-sounding title. Before we begin to work with student responses to this text, it might be useful to address this issue of tedium (a Latin word for "boring"), since it is a problem that students frequently seem to face when dealing with lengthy or unusual-looking texts.

We have also found that when our students have been asked to explain what they mean by "boredom," they are unable to. Nor are they able to agree on the features of the text they are reading that makes it boring. In a way, this makes sense: The word "boring" tends to be heavily coded. That is, it tends to have special significance for the one who uses it. (We also use **coded language** when we say that something is "positive" or "negative," or that we "like" it.) But its special significance is not immediately apparent to others.

Try defining what the term "boring" means to you and the kinds of texts you would classify under its heading. You could begin with what we have already referred to as a "privative definition": that is, you could begin considering what is *not* boring. Next, compare your definitions with those of your classmates. Can you detect similarities? What kinds of words do you all use to define boredom? Are they nouns? Are they verbs? What difference might their being nouns or verbs make? What are some causes of boredom?

One of us in a first-year writing course regularly teaches a book titled *The Education of Henry Adams,* written by Henry Adams and published at the beginning of the twentieth century. It is a rather long text (approximately five hundred pages, depending on the edition), replete with historical references, written in a highly complex and (in many students' eyes) repetitive style. Students unanimously classified it as "boring," at least initially. When they were asked to explain why they find it boring, they said: it is packed with historical details; it reflects on "education" (a topic that for many students brings to mind images of rote memorization and cramped seating); it lacks "action," "adventure," or "romance," or other "entertaining" elements; it is not written for an "average reader," since it describes an unusual kind of life to which few students believe at first they can relate. As Nangula Shejvali explains: "Upon first sight, I was presented with several opportunities to form the notion that *The Education of Henry Adams* was a boring book—and a book that is believed to be boring immediately becomes difficult to read."

What Shejvali said suggests that "boredom" might be a word for difficulties that are acknowledged as such as well as for those that may not be. In either case, what does boredom have to do with the time it takes to read a text and with a reader's difficulty in holding its details in mind? Possibly a great deal. That is why readers invent different strategies, such as writing, to keep their attention focused on the abundance of details characteristic of longer texts. Writing—whether in the form of a Difficulty Paper, a journal, textual annotations, or note-taking—can be a capacious safety (saving) net.

In their reading of *The Education of Henry Adams*, for example, the students we referred to earlier found that they could even alleviate their boredom by deciding, with the help of a highlighter or pen, which textual features to place in "light" and which to leave in "shadow." Highlighting and underlining are themselves forms of writing. They are also forms of activity. And since activity relieves boredom, their decision to pay attention to the text by drawing this kind of distinction—light/shadow—eased their distress.

Introducing *The Rime of the Ancyent Marinere*

Since *Marinere* is a well-known poem, frequently anthologized and taught in high school and college courses, it is possible you may already have read it. Even if not, you may be familiar with pieces of it, for it has entered the popular repertoire—the public consciousness—in different ways. Many are familiar with the elderly and crazy-eyed sailor who obsessively shares his tale of his shooting of an albatross. Many have heard of such sayings as "All creatures great and small" (the Bible is the original source); "Water, water everywhere . . . "; and "I carry an albatross around my neck." Poems such as the *Marinere* make their presence felt—even when one has not read them—in the way they are talked about, transmitted, and referred to. In either case, whether you are conscious of it or not, you may have prior knowledge of the text (as part of your repertoire) that will set up certain kinds of expectations about it.

Where to Begin with a Longer Text

Keep in mind what you just wrote as you read the following student responses to the *Marinere.* These responses were produced in a class called English 205: Literary Questions, taught by Professor Bianca Falbo of Lafayette College, as part of the following assignment:

> On the basis of your notes and your reflections on them [editors' note: Falbo is referring here to the Double-Entry Notebook that preceded this assignment], write a one-page single-spaced paper in which you describe the difficulties you have encountered with Coleridge's text. I expect this paper to reflect your thoughtful and sustained engagement with the text, especially with those moments in the text that for one reason or another puzzle and confuse you, leave you with questions, or otherwise frustrate, undermine, or complicate your process of interpretation. If the difficulties you encounter are numerous, rather than listing all of them, narrow your focus by isolating and discussing specifically one or two examples from the text of what you take to be the major interpretive problems with which you are confronted. Be prepared to discuss your response to both parts of the assignment in class.

As you read through the responses, consider what kinds of difficulties they identify and what kind of work each writer is doing.

While reading *The Rime of the Ancyent Marinere,* I was extremely confused with what the author was trying to say. There were several words that he expressed that confused me, because I was unable to know who he was referring to. I was mostly confused in part two because it was the part that set the stage for the rest of the rime, and without understanding that, the rest was confusing . . . Phrases and terms used in part two also confused me because I was not clear on the vocabulary or what the term related to . . . The author used Old English and I misunderstood meanings and interpretations because of that. (Trisha Zeytoonjian)

I found reading Part III of *The Rime of the Ancyent Marinere* extremely difficult. One of my main questions is whether the ghost of the Albatross is haunting this sailor or if he has just gone insane. I am not sure if this is something the reader is supposed to know or if the reader is supposed to wonder about this . . . Another major difficulty I had with this poem was the use of the pronouns "her" and "his" . . . Whose ribs, bones, and lips does the sailor see? (Elizabeth Darcy)

Both these readers single out as a difficulty the poem's unclear references; they do not know what certain words are referring to. They also mention problems of vocabulary caused by the poem's use of "Old English." (*Rime* intentionally reproduces older linguistic forms to lend the poem an archaic flavor, and it recirculates an old genre—the ballad.) They are quite right. A writer's use of unfamiliar language can often make a reader feel that a work is inaccessible or impossible to understand. But these readers also mention problems related to the poem's presentation of incidents, its sequencing, overall design—difficulties that the text's length seem to exacerbate. Trisha Zeytoonjian is concerned that her inability to understand one of the poem's parts, one whose function is to "set the stage," will impede her understanding of the next part of the poem. She anticipates future difficulty. Elizabeth Darcy points out that the poem does not make clear what it expects the reader "to know" or "to wonder about."

Think about this: Both writers experience difficulties not because they do not know, but *because of what they know*. What they know, in general and about reading, sets up certain expectations about the workings of language (remember the "grammatical" reader earlier in the chapter?) and of genre that do not seem to be applicable to the present task. For example, Zeytoonjian considers "setting the stage," a term that brings **drama** to mind. And Darcy expects Coleridge to stipulate to a reader directly what he or she needs to know or to think about—an expectation more appropriate for **thesis statements** than poems.

Navigating the Water: Kristin Pontoski

How, then, does a reader engage these difficulties while navigating the waters (an appropriate metaphor for the *Marinere*) of a long text and keeps herself from being left behind? Let us look at how another student, Kristin Pontoski, worked with this challenging text. Pontoski, like Darcy and Zeytoonijan, focuses on only one section of the poem, and she identifies the same kinds of problems. What does she do that helps her move beyond them? What can we learn from what she does?

Reading Coleridge's *The Rime of the Ancyent Marinere* left me with an abundance of questions. The complicated language, ambiguous pronouns, and unusual metaphors forced me to reread the poem multiple times to merely understand what the text was saying before I could actually start to think about what the text meant. I had to consult *Webster's Dictionary* and the *Oxford English Dictionary* for definitions of words and for clues to what a word might have meant hundreds of years ago. Once I got a better idea of the basic language of the poem, however, I still struggled to make sense of the text. As I was reading, Part III struck me as the most difficult section of the poem to understand because I could not tell whether the Marinere's descriptions were real or hallucinated.

I was confused throughout all of Part III about the mysterious ship that the Marinere saw. In lines 147–48, there are several descriptive words—"didg'd, plung'd, tack'd, and veer'd"—that would suggest movement. However, other parts of the poem made me think that the ship was not actually moving at all . . . This makes it seem to me like the Marinere is imagining its movement . . . This idea is further expressed when he says, "How fast she neres and neres!/Are those *her* Sails that glance in the Sun/Like restless gossamers?" (III. 174–76). I was particularly confused with the word "gossamers." According to the dictionary, it means some kind of web-like, light, and filmy substance . . . Throughout the poem, Coleridge uses masculine pronouns to describe the sun and feminine pronouns to describe the ship. These pronoun sequences are often hard to follow. Plus, the extensive personification makes it difficult to concentrate on the objects that Coleridge actually describes.

So, is this ship real or is it the Marinere's imagination? This question is made even more unclear with the introduction of the apparent crew members of this ship. I don't understand where the "woman and her Fleshless Pheere" (lll. 180) come from . . . This confusion goes back to my original question about the pronouns. It is difficult to determine whether Coleridge talks about people or objects . . .

The ship leaves as quickly as it had appeared and, despite the wind that came up behind it, still shows no signs of actually being driven through the water: "With never a whisper in the Sea/Off darts the Spectre-ship" (lll. 199–200). Therefore, I get the impression that the Marinere made up the whole scene.

Although my close analysis of this part of the poem has helped me to understand it better than some of the other parts, I am still quite confused. The language that the Marinere chooses is difficult and often ambiguous. Plus, it is hard to determine what the Marinere means based on the context of the poem because he uses so many metaphors. I realize that each strange capitalization and unusual use or placement of a word probably has some significance to the story, but studying this section has not helped me to completely understand this significance. My interpretation of the mysterious ship and its two crew members is hazy at best, but perhaps Coleridge writes it like that purposely so that the reader has to decide whether anything that the Marinere describes is real or imaginary.

Pontoski states at the end that she stills feels very confused about the poem. And yet, her writing displays a great deal of understanding. She is able to hold her reading problems at a critical distance. She keeps moving through the text, as if aware and comfortable with the fact that not everything can be entirely clear. Her reading slows down at times, but it never stalls completely. As she says in her opening paragraph, she felt she had to reread the poem several times, and she knew that she had to consult the dictionary. But these two moves—while effective—only take her so far.

What she does next is especially interesting. She starts playing with words, establishing patterns that rearrange the connections between isolated words and that activate implicit (not fully developed) meanings. She notices that certain words suggest movement while others do not. "Sun" is repeatedly referred to in masculine terms, "ship" in feminine terms. She expands these words, these **symbols,** into potential stories. Eventually, the stories (explanations) she begins to weave around "sun" and "ship" lead her to conclude that the Marinere is himself confused, that he may be hallucinating. This marks an important stage in her reading. She understands that the confusion she feels is not a marker of her deficiency as a reader but an effect of the text itself. She is not the cause of that confusion. She is feeling the confusion the narrator's tale is producing. Her confusion is actually a sign of her sensitivity to the text. It is caused by what she knows about the ways in which these symbols are commonly used to convey clues, information, and meanings.

Can you recall any reading experiences in which your confusion could be attributed to the text's narrative viewpoint, to what seemed to you the narrator's unreliability? Why might a text deliberately provoke confusion? (Remember Elizabeth Bishop's poem?)

Let us return to Pontoski: She is able to manage the difficulties generated both by the text and her expectations about it, by employing certain moves, moves that had in all likelihood served her well before. For example, she searches for and establishes patterns, which means that she is able to keep herself reading even when she might not understand the significance of a detail in isolation. This is a critical point: She does not stop when something is unclear; she keeps moving; she seems to know that the understanding of a text unfolds in time. In addition, rather than dismiss her reactions, she trusts them, recognizing that their source is the text rather than her own inabilities.

Recuperating the Past

Perhaps a reader of Pontoski's work might conclude that by choosing to create a contemporary and "relevant" pathway through a historically remote text she has misread it, in serious ways. Should we agree that she has produced an erroneous historical reading? Not necessarily. Or, maybe, not at first.

At times of uncertainty like this, it can be helpful to consult what "expert" readers and critics have to say. Speaking of Michel Montaigne, a sixteenth-century essayist we consider in Chapter 6, Richard Regosin, a literary critic, makes the following comment:

> The critic can and should attempt to be faithful to the intellectual, cultural, and literary context with which Montaigne wrote, to the ideas that shaped his attitudes toward writing, to his own readings, and to the contemporary meanings of words and concepts. Yet there are no means for recuperating the past in any absolute sense, no means for engaging it that are not themselves readings and interpretations incapable of fully overcoming the gap of historical differences (Regosin, 9).

While critics may need to consider a text's historical horizons, not every reader need turn that consideration of history into an opportunity—or obstacle. At least, not when other difficulties beg his or her attention. Pontoski's decision to bracket certain considerations, to foreground some issues and place others in the background, can be a very helpful strategy for readers to employ when they are working through long and complex texts. Not every element need be accorded equal weight. Not every element can be attended to at any one moment (think of those students we mentioned earlier who placed some textual elements in the light, others in the shadow). But numerous elements can receive such attention in subsequent, **recursive readings.** Once more elements are understood, more elements can be engaged simultaneously.

Reading the Hybrid Text

So far in this chapter, we have explored the kinds of difficulties that are posed by a text's length and the duration of a reading. We have also examined how a text's apparent "confusion" can become more manageable when considered a quality of the text itself, rather than a reflection of "poor reading." In fact, as we saw in the example of Potonski's work, she is a quite capable reader. At this point, we want to examine a new kind of difficulty, related to the presence of multiple, and at times seemingly contradictory, generic clues. The problem is one we label **hybridity.**

We begin with two new responses to Coleridge's poem:

Coleridge's "The Rime of the Ancyent Marinere" is a very frustrating piece. The text is filled with complications that make the story hard to interpret." (Kelly Maiers)

Thus far, I have found "The Rime of the Ancyent Marinere" to be a little more than confusing. This is most likely because it is not straightforward; it does not tell us exactly what things represent or signify, or even the chronological order or importance of the events that are taking place. (Idara Umoren)

What kind of reader expectations trigger Maiers' and Umoren's difficulties? Umoren finds the poem "confusing" because it doesn't tell us its "chronological order or importance." Maiers says that "the text is filled with complications that make the story hard to interpret." Are they identifying the same difficulty?

Whether they are or not, they seem to agree that something is awry in the poem's presentation of "story." Maiers says so directly; Umoren speaks of "chronological order" and "events that are taking place." But why are they focusing on these narrative elements? The *Marinere*, after all, would seem to be an example of poetry, not narrative. Why do these readers react in this way? What reading issues are at stake in their reaction?

It might be useful for you to pause for a moment to think about the issue of "story." Once again, we want you to reflect on your pre-existing knowledge, your repertoire. In Chapter 4, we will focus on narrative elements in detail (if you want to turn now to that chapter for assistance, we encourage you to do so), but at the moment we are speaking of an understanding of story that seems fundamental, possibly even universal. In fact, the critic J. Hills Miller even says that "Nothing seems more natural and universal to human beings than telling stories. Surely there is no human culture, however 'primitive,' without its stories and habits of storytelling, its myths of the origin of the world, its legends of the tribe or groups of stories about folk heroes . . . From our earlier childhood we hear stories and learn to repeat them" (*Critical Terms for Literary Study*, 66). As J. Hills Miller explains, the human capacity to tell stories is one way men and women collectively build a significant and orderly world around themselves (*Critical Terms*, 69). Human beings often cope with the difficulties of existence by transforming problems into stories with beginnings, middles, and ends. Stories can be ways of both managing and interpreting difficulties.

With these ideas in mind, let us return to the student texts. In posing questions about story and chronology, the writers are actually picking up and responding to the work's "blurry-ing" effect. And we delight in what they see, since many literary critics have composed rich interpretations of this feature of the text. *Marinere* is both a poem and a story. In fact, it is often categorized as "narrative poetry" because it presents elements (markers) of those two genres as well as others: smaller poetic forms such as the ballad and the kind of dialogue (the Marinere speaks; the wedding guest replies, when he can) found not only in story but in drama. Look again at the terms Maiers and Umoren have used in discussing *Marinere:* that the "story [is] hard to interpret," that it does not present events in "chronological order." Their use of such terms suggests they have perceived that this text, like most texts, is a hybrid, a *fusion of genres,* which as such can produce confusion.

But what does this mean? What is a hybrid? What makes readers recognize it as such? And once they do, how do they move from recognizing hybridity (the fusion of genres or elements) to understanding its effects (con-fusion)? To answer, let us return for a moment to the ideas about genre we mentioned in the introduction, and build on them.

Understanding Genre

As we initially discussed, genre can be understood as a "frame of reference," a "set of historical and cultural conventions." Genre is a category, a way to group together texts with common features. The contemporary theorist/philosopher Jacques Derrida explains that a genre can be used to **legitimize** new ways of writing by providing them with a name and a way to be recognized. He refers to "the law of genre," explaining that a genre constitutes itself by establishing "norms and interdictions" (notice the legal language): that is, a set of conditions, prescriptions, prohibitions, limits, and exclusions (for example, a particular kind of poem is a sonnet because it contains certain kinds of features but not others). A genre also constitutes itself as a practice that establishes and disseminates (spreads) common knowledge, knowledge to be shared. (If you think about an example of a newly established musical genre, what Derrida says might sound less daunting.) Since the boundaries between genres can be fluid and permeable, one writer's use of a genre might differ from that of another writer's. One reader's understanding of genre might also differ from that of another reader, depending on how each interprets its "laws." And definitions of a genre might even change over time.

The "law" that Derrida talks about, therefore, is as often violated (transgressed) as it is observed. This means that every text is generically "impure"; every text is a hybrid, quilting together elements of different genres. Whether a text is labeled in terms of one category rather than another may very well be based on a reader's interpretation, and on his or her assessment of which of its features are dominant. For example, while the *Marinere* may be classified as "narrative poetry," some readers might focus more on its "poetic" elements, others its "narrative" qualities.

Another way to think about hybridity that our students have found helpful is through the critical lens provided by a different term, **intertextuality.** The following definition by M.H. Abrams summarizes how it is commonly understood, and it makes us reflect on how the intertextual nature of written texts affects reading:

> The term *intertextuality,* popularized especially by literary critic and theorist Julia Kristeva, is used to signify the multiple ways in which any one literary text is made up of other texts, by means of its open or covert citations and *allusions,* its repetitions and transformations of the formal and substantive features of earlier texts, or simply its unavoidable participation in the common stock of linguistic and literary conventions that are "always already" in place and constitute the discourses into which we are born (317).

But the statement also suggests that "intertextuality" is a characteristic of all texts, not just literary texts. (Think again about a genre—in music, literature, pop culture, dance—which you know well and reflect on how it too is "made up of other texts.")

Viewing Your Own Writing as Hybrid Genre

We have introduced these brief passages from Derrida and Abrams to call attention to the fact that the kind of textual conflicts and tensions our students notice as they read and remark upon in their difficulty papers are the very phenomena that different theorists have addressed in different ways. But unlike these more experienced readers, students glide over their difficulties; they leave behind the possibility of making astute theoretical observations about the texts they read.

We would now like you to think about how your own writing might be read as a hybrid genre, or an intertext. In other words, we would like you to think about the ways in which your writing partakes of the qualities that philosophers of language and literary theorists study.

Select a piece of your writing. Look at the words you use. Can you identify them as terms that belong to a particular genre? A dictionary of literary terms, such as that of Abrams', might help you here. In the previous chapter we used the term "repertoire." How does it relate to genre? Might your writing be blurring different genres together? Might your text be read intertextually, as a location, a page where other texts you have read or heard converge? Might your text be multi-voiced, that is, might it speak differently, reproducing the language of your family at some moments, the language of different academic or popular discourses at others? Think of whether a teacher has ever commented on your use of cliché or slang. How might you reframe such comments using the notion of intertext?

We understand that the work we have just asked you to do may be especially challenging. But even if you do not think you were particularly successful at performing it—and our sense is that you probably did much better than you think—consider how thinking about a text in terms of its hybridity and intertextuality, rather than homogeneity, can affect the way you read it. And consider how framing a text as hybrid and multi-voiced might make you rethink the concept of "original genius," or a writer's **"intention."** Within the framework of intertextuality, how much control over language do we really have as readers or as writers?

Reading as Rewriting: Patrick Beh-Forrest

To bring this chapter to a close, we present one final Difficulty Paper on *The Rime of the Ancyent Marinere,* written by Patrick Beh-Forrest. We present this essay free of questions and guiding terms, as we ask you to read it in terms of the categories we have provided. How does Patrick Beh-Forrest both articulate these barriers and overcome them. What kinds of understandings are implicit in his writing? What are the moves he makes as a reader, as a thinker. To what extent does his reading of the poem represent a rewriting of it?

Although I have read "The Rime of the Ancyent Marinere" several times over the course of my education, it continues to be a challenge to interpret. This difficulty stems from two major sources. The first of these is the language itself, as it is of a time unfamiliar to me, and the second is a problem common to most works of literature I have studied, namely the complex imagery of the work.

The first of these problems, the language itself, is readily apparent in all sections of the poem, and very much so in the third book of the poem. The first and most obvious difference from modern writing is the capitalization of some words of the poem. This occurs in the very first line of Book III, as the Marinere relates, "I saw a something in the Sky" (III, 139). At first it seems that this was similar to the German language, which capitalizes all nouns, but that theory is refuted on the very next line, which states "No bigger than my fist;" (III, 140). So I am left to believe that there is some greater significance to this emphasis on certain nouns, and I am unsure what to make of them.

The confined form of the poem also leads to much confusion. Since the poem is written in iambic meter, lines are often phrased in confusing ways to fit that meter, and the need for rhyme further complicates the poem, as is seen here:

> She doth not tack from side to side-
> Hither to work us weal
> Without wind, withouten tide
> She steddies with upright keel. (III, 159–163).

While words such as "doth," "hither," "withouten," and "steddies" are known or immediately apparent to me, they serve to frustrate and hinder me, making it harder to attack the most confusing phrase, "work us weal." Thus I am almost forced to rewrite the poem in language I understand so that I might work on the important sections.

Far worse than the actual mechanics of the poem, however, is the subject of the poem. Book III contains an excellent example of this in the appearance of the woman and her companion on the ghost ship. The entire book is concerned with this specter and its effect on the crew, and yet I am still unclear of the events that transpire.

As before, the typography of the poem struck the first blow for confusion, this time with italicized pronouns. The first occurrence, "Are those *her* that glance in the Sun" (III, 175), gives way to many more, and the pattern of meaning remains elusive. Initially I hoped that all the pronouns referring to the lady and her companion would be emphasized, but that was hope proved false by "That woman and her fleshless Pheere" (III, 180). Then I thought that perhaps the emphasis only appeared when the Marinere described physical attributes, but I was doubly wrong, as seen in "Her skin is as white as leprosy" (III, 187) and "Her flesh makes the still air cold" (III, 190).

Beyond this relatively simple problem of presentation lies the mysterious pair themselves. I do not know whom the woman and her companion represent. "And she is far liker Death than he;" (III, 189) makes me wonder if perhaps she is in fact Death, and he is her companion. This would seem to be supported by the demise of the sailors following her statement "The Game is done! I've won, I've won!" (III, 193) and subsequent departure, and thus perhaps the emphasis on the pronouns is explained. If she truly were death, then the Marinere would have good reason to speak of her in such awed and reverent tones.

Still, the companion is less clear. Why does her victory over him lead to the deaths of the sailors? Why is her description in the present tense and his in the past, as seen in "*His* bones were black with many a crack," (III, 181) and "*Her* lips are red, *her* looks are free," (III, 186)? What does the following passage mean?

> A gust of wind sterte up behind
> And whistled thro' his bones;
> Thro' the holes of his eyes and the hole of his mouth
> Half-whistles and half groans (III, 195–99)

Based on the fact that this passage precedes the departure of the ghost ship, I believe it possible that the man is the ship itself. However, this leads to other problems. Why does the ghost ship need wind to depart, but not to arrive? What is the significance of the "horned Moon" that rises as the ship leaves? Surely this refers to a crescent moon, but the association of horns with infernal beings is impossible to ignore.

If Book III, only 76 lines and one of the shortest sections of the book, confounds me so, what does that bode for the remainder of the poem?

Taking Stock

- Make a list of the new terms we have introduced in this chapter.
- Take a look at that list. If you now understand those terms—or some of them—differently, and you must if you have engaged this process of learning, how would you describe that change? What caused it?
- Which of the terms you entered in your Triple-Entry Notebook is getting more attention from you? Why? Which of the columns is easier or more difficult to write in?
- What has changed in the moves you make as a reader, writer, and thinker?
- When do you find yourself thinking most intensely—when you read or when you write?
- Do you think "differently" when you read and when you write?
- What might you add to your "literacy narrative," having worked through this chapter?
- Add to, revise, or rewrite the paragraphs of instruction/advice you addressed to the student in the previous chapter. What would you want him or her to know that earlier you were not aware might be helpful? As you addressed that student earlier, what did you not take into account that you might/should have?
- As we addressed you so far, what did we not take into account that we might/should have?
- We promise to include the most fruitful suggestions any of you make in our future revision of this book.

Retrospective

In this chapter, which focused on a longer text, *The Ancyent Marinere,* a text we also classified a "hybrid," we explored new difficulties and the strategies for confronting them. We paid particular attention to the idea of readers' transferring familiar knowledge into new contexts, and the "mismatch" that may occur when what readers expect is different than what texts seem to offer. We also considered the challenges created by long texts, boring texts, and texts that issue mixed cues.

And what did we learn about managing these challenges from our student readers? By writing about and reflecting on their difficulties, they were able to discover the techniques they already possessed for unraveling and putting together components of complex texts. They also discovered the value of suspending their desire for instant clarity, learning instead that meaning unfolds (or is constructed) in time and that the momentum of a reading may be maintained by placing conundrums temporarily in "shadow." They learned to trust their initial reactions as effects of the text, and to substitute for the question of "Why can't I figure out what this means?" that of "Why does this text create confusion at this point?" And they learned to move forward in their reading of an historically remote text by placing issues of historical determination in the background, at least temporarily, in order to engage a work in terms of their lived experience as contemporary readers.

4

Intermezzo

> Intermezzo: A short movement separating the major sections of a lengthy musical composition or work
>
> —*The American Heritage Dictionary*

In many musical compositions, an intermezzo is used to mark a division between two major parts of a work. Sometimes it functions to call attention to the different direction the work will take; sometimes it establishes connections between the two parts. Invariably, the intermezzo does things a bit differently, in terms of tone, theme, and subject matter (these are terms applicable to writing as well as to music). In a musical or dramatic performance, an intermezzo is also a break in the action. The audience gets up and goes out to the hall for a drink, a chat, an opportunity to comment on the performance and to have a look around.

We imagine this chapter as an intermezzo of sorts: a link between the previous chapters and the next ones. In this chapter, we do a close reading of the work Susan Connelly does as she learns to identify and transform difficulty into a tool of understanding.

We have debated whether or not to reproduce sections of the text she is responding to, Carolyn Steedman's *Landscape for a Good Woman*. But, ultimately, we have opted not to do so for the following reason: Often, students claim they have difficulty reading texts that refer to other texts when those other texts are inaccessible to them. Our counterclaim is that sometimes not having access to those other texts can help readers focus more pointedly on the moves a writer makes as she carves a space in her writing for the absent text she is evoking and engaging. Rather than feeling cut off by a writer's quotation from an unknown source, a reader might ask: Why would this writer rely on this quotation? What does the writer's turn to another text indicate in her argument? How does this writer present the ideas of another? How does she introduce them? What kind of work does she do before and after the quotation? And how does the quotation stand in relation to the rest of the writer's text? These questions are productive and may induce a reader to pay closer attention to the conventions of quotation. And it is precisely *because* the reader is unfamiliar with the quoted material and has no specific investment in it that he or she may be able to ask these questions in the first place.

As we shift your attention from Steedman to Connelly, we ask that you examine and analyze Connelly's attempts at interpreting *Landscape*. But as we do that, we want to point out that her observations and perceptions, as astute and insightful as they are, are nevertheless typical of students *who learn to trust* the value of their explorations of difficulty, sustained in their efforts by the validation those explorations receive from their teachers and peers.

Connelly's text forges a transition for us from reading poetry to reading **prose.** The threads we carry over from the last chapter are "narrative" and "storytelling."

Moving from Poetry to Prose

> [In] prose, everything is provided by the author. The setting is thoroughly described and every point of the story is told in detail, taking the reader from the beginning to the end. To understand the writing, the reader must only go through the text, looking up unfamiliar words in the dictionary, and the rest is laid out by the author. If the reader does not understand part of the story, or missed an underlying theme, then she must reread it until it is understood.
>
> —Susan Connelley

> Prose n.: 1. Ordinary speech or writing, as distinguished from verse. 2. Commonplace expression or quality. [ME < OFr < Lat *prosa (oratio)*, straightforward (discourse) < *proversus*, p.part. of *provertere*, to turn forward : *pro*, forward + *vertere*, to turn]
>
> —*The American Heritage Dictionary*

> Prose n.: straightforward discourse 1a. the ordinary form of written or spoken language, without metrical structure. Opposed to *poetry, verse, rime,* or *metre.* 1b. a piece of prose, as opp. to a poem; a composition in prose; a prose exercise. 1c. a (prose) story or narrative. 2. plain, simple, matter of fact, (and hence) dull or commonplace expression, quality, spirit, etc. (the opposite of poetry).
>
> —*The Oxford English Dictionary*

In this Intermezzo we make a transition from poetry to prose. This book is written in prose. So are (most) folktales, soap operas, diaries, cartoons, confessions, films, documentaries, biographies, autobiographies, movie reviews, situation comedies, and so on. Prose uses the kind of language with which you are probably most familiar, the language you employ in conversation, e-mails, jokes, anecdotes, lab reports, and writing assignments. According to the first dictionary definition at the beginning of the chapter, prose is "Ordinary speech or writing, as distinguished from verse . . . [It has a] commonplace expression or quality."

Ordinary. Commonplace. Unlike poetry. Given these qualities, you may think that we are moving from a more difficult genre to a less difficult one. In many instances, the language of prose is indeed less difficult than that of poetry. Theorist Viktor Shklovsky, for example, in accord with dictionary definitions, says that prose is "ordinary speech . . . economical, easy, proper; the goddess of prose (*dea prosae*) is a goddess of the accurate, facile type, of the 'direct' expression of a child" (Rivkin and Ryan, 22). Significantly, although our student Susan Connelly had not read Shklovsky's definition of prose, she similarly suggested that prose possesses a natural kind of clarity; that in prose, everything is laid out, or should be. In her opinion, all a reader of prose should have to do is read [the text], follow [it] along. If the language of poetry is, as Shklovsky explains, "a difficult, roughened, impeded language" (22)—the kind of language that must be struggled with and unpacked—the language of prose, in contrast, seems to speak for itself. It is tractable, accessible, familiar.

But it is also the case that certain kinds of prose complicate these definitions. They complicate them; they do not invalidate them. Even writers who most blatantly transgress the rules, in the very effort to expand and revise the possibilities for understanding what prose offers (the argument is valid for any other genre as well), must inevitably rely on them. There is no transgression without something to transgress. No transformation without something to transform. That "something," that nugget of commonplace, shared understanding of a genre, is what provides readers with a base, a starting point, that can make them notice and assess the different kinds of reading the difficulties they are experiencing call for.

As usual, we approach this area of investigation by examining how a student in a first-year composition course, Susan Connelly, learned to identify and work through the difficulties she encountered as she read a particularly demanding work of prose, *Landscape for a Good Woman*. In the following section, we provide a close reading of a set of Difficulty Papers she produced.

Surveying the Landscape

Landscape for a Good Woman, by Carolyn Steedman, is a very difficult book to read. It is an elaborate record of the author's attempt to understand how her life has been shaped by her mother's, father's, and siblings' lives and how all their lives in turn have been shaped by other lives and by the economic and historical circumstances in which they lived. To gain this understanding, Steedman deploys various interpretive frameworks—sociological, psychoanalytical, folkloric, autobiographical, and biographical. She relies on the work of others—critics, theorists, writers—and, by means of several scholarly conventions—epigraphs, footnotes, literary allusions, quotations—she offers her readers the insights these works/authors provided her. She stretches the properties of prose to try to convey the story of her life in the form of a case study. As you might infer, the book requires a lot of interpretive work from its readers: They must establish connections among diverse materials, and shift from one generic **paradigm** (psychoanalysis, for example) to another (sociology), each with its own interpretive conventions.

Connelly's writing captures some of the difficulties of doing that. We will reproduce excerpts from a sequence of Difficulty Papers in which she "tried to get the meaning of the book," and in so doing, learned to identify and actualize the "reading instructions" Steedman provides for the readers of her text.

Connelly's first move is to draw a working definition of prose:

> When reading prose, everything is provided by the author. The setting is thoroughly described and every point of the story is told in detail, taking the reader from the beginning to the end. To understand

the writing, the reader must only go through the text, looking up unfamiliar words in the dictionary, and the rest is laid out by the author. If the reader does not understand part of the story, or missed an underlying theme, then she must re-read it until it is understood.

Notice how similar Connelly's definition of prose is to the dictionary definition we have cited at the beginning of the chapter. Perhaps the most intriguing feature Connelly assigns to prose, a feature that reveals a lot about why she thinks she can read prose the way she does, is its straightforwardness, or its forward movement. In addition to suggesting clarity, lack of ambiguity, and abundance of details, Connelly's formulation of prose suggests that writers (can) use it to carry a story, a meaning, a proposition, a narrative, a chronology, a temporal sequence *forward*, with appropriate links and props to sustain it. (Indeed, this is very possible. But consider the alternative possibilities that writers must give up.)

Our brief description of Steedman's narrative method should alert you to the kinds of difficulties a reader who approaches this text with such expectations about prose's forwardness, and a writer's control of story, will experience. In Connelly's case, additional difficulties stem from her assumptions about the different ways in which prose works in **case studies** and in life narratives (see Chapter 6)—two of the several prose sub-genres Steedman deploys.

This is what we see Connelly doing. We see her begin to work with what she knows or assumes about prose. Having laid down her provisional framework for reading prose/narrative, vis-à-vis Steedman's text, she experiences and identifies one of the difficulties generated by the mismatch between her assumptions and the text's demands. Although the self-examination that leads to it is not spelled out in her writing, we see her making adjustments and revisions that enable her to notice and eventually respond to (engage) the ways in which Carolyn Steedman uses case-study genre to catch the tangle of stories and forces that shaped her life. Not an easy task. But that Connelly should recognize that she cannot readily tap into Steedman's life, which cannot be conventionally narrated, is a sign of perceptive reading. Connelly writes:

In the first section of Steedman's "Landscape," [pp.1–24] I found it extremely difficult to understand the formal tone she uses. Steedman writes: "the written case-study allows the writer to enter the present into the past, allows the dream, the wish or the fantasy of the past to shape current time, and treats them as evidence of their own right" (21). This excerpt shows that Steedman becomes an outsider looking in, detached from her present writing, in the form of a case study. The case-study method of writing allows her to move away from the typical writings of a working-class mother-daughter relationship. But since Steedman uses the "feeling of being on the outside" (9) to explain the story, it is difficult for me, as a reader, to relate to the being behind the formal case study.

As I continued reading Steedman's "Stories," I came across the word "landscape" [which was subsequently] used on several occasions throughout the book. I could not figure out what "landscape" was supposed to represent. I decided to look the word up in the *American Heritage Dictionary* and I found out that it meant "a picture depicting a view." From this information I gathered that Steedman would be using the formal tone "to depict a view" into her life. Steedman, like Lynn Emanuel (author of *The Dig*) would be using "bits and pieces" (21) of writing to form a picture of her life in the reader's mind.

The first difficulty Connelly identifies has to do with "the formal tone [Steedman] uses." The sentence is ambiguous. It is not clear whether she has difficulty understanding the choice or the effect of the formal **tone.** The paragraph records that confusion. She seems to think that the case study suppresses the "dream, the wish, or the fantasy"; that the detached, looking-in stance of the writer is a strategy of rejection, allowing her "to move away from the typical writings of a working-class mother-daughter relationship." This kind of writing about lives does not seem to interest her. But look at what happens at the end of the paragraph. She specifies her difficulty at the same time that she justifies/explains it as her alienation from the narrator ("the being"), a consequence of the writer's deliberate choice of genre and style. And throughout the paragraph, we can perceive how Connelly herself is an "outsider looking in, detached from her present writing." Is she not understanding? Or understanding too well and perhaps not liking what she is asked to understand?

Interestingly, a bit later, that detachment provides a perspective on—an interesting "view" of—the difficulty. As she continues writing, she tells of the search for meaning that her confusion at the recurrence of the word "landscape" triggered. The "look-it-up-in-the-dictionary" strategy, which she clearly reaches out to on her own, leads her to construct an interesting meaning. That meaning is not a simple transposition of the dictionary definition into her thinking: It is the result of how she interprets that definition in light of her emerging revised understanding of prose. Prose, as a form of writing in which the setting is thoroughly described and every point of the story is told in detail, cedes space to prose as a form of writing that comes in bits and pieces, and as such, requires a different engagement from the reader. At this point, as if to support her interpretation, she branches back to and "cites" a prior reading experience—the reading of a collection of poems (*The Dig*) by Lynn Emanuel, which had required she learn to read each poem as a bit or piece of a "story" she, the reader, had to construct. Her understanding of her difficulty—its causes and the work they call for—becomes insightful, bolder, and carries her along through a "landscape" she can now negotiate on her own. This is what she writes:

> In part two of Carolyn Kay Steedman's *Landscape*, I found it difficult but interesting that certain topics were referred to again from part one. On page 30, Steedman refers to "bits and pieces" again, as she did on page 21. I am sure now that Steedman's story will be coming through to the readers in bits and pieces, just like Lynn Emanuel's poetry (or a variation of the fragmental work). The story Steedman tells is also from many points of view, sometimes her story, sometimes her mother's, sometimes other accounts of what a working class family during a certain time period experienced. These different points of view become a difficulty themselves when it (she?) switches often.

"I found it difficult *but* interesting. . . . " Being able to consider some of her difficulties with "interest" marks an important moment in her approach to reading, in her "story of reading." It marks her awareness that what she "does not get" with ease might deserve, and reward her for, more work. But what does "more work" actually mean? Re-reading in and of itself does not necessarily lead to understanding. What does, then?

You might be intrigued to know—as we are—that "interest" comes from the Latin *interesse. Interesse* means "to be in the middle," "to be among." In the beginning, Connelly's initial understanding of "formal tone" as distancing both explained and justified her difficulty: She explained that the formal tone kept her from reaching out to (making direct contact with) the characters because their actions and thoughts came to her through the filter of the "case-study" language. As we said earlier, she had the same stance toward the text she was reading that she thought Steedman had toward the text she wrote: looking in from the outside. In the excerpt below we see her forging a way of "connecting" with the text that allows her to read the story from within it. Remarkably, that connection grows out of a moment that had initially puzzled her—her difficulty understanding why Steedman would refer to her mother as a "good mother."

I found this intriguing because in the context of the story it seems as though Steedman uses the "good mother" as a form of irony. She is not literally a good mother (but what is a good mother anyway) but is a good mother because of the sacrifices she faced in order to take care of the family.

Connelly ponders: Since Steedman portrays her mother as tough, unsentimental, even self-absorbed, is she ironic when she calls her a "good mother"? If Steedman is indeed ironic, reading her **irony** from within the landscape, Connelly can nevertheless call on other perspectives—that of the mother herself, of other characters—to decide how to interpret Steedman's "intriguing" appellative.

In the remainder of the Difficulty Paper, Connelly identifies yet another (major) feature of the book that halts and complicates straightforward reading. This is a difficulty that scholarly texts, texts that quote or borrow from other works for support or to set up a particular argument, often raise for readers unaccustomed to this style.

Connelly mentions instances in which Steedman tries to "express her feelings to the reader" by referencing specific works, as when she refers to "X" as the "Southern version of *The Road to Wigan Pier.*" Unless the reader has read this work, she writes, "the reader cannot possibly understand what the book has to do in relation with the way she is feeling. I could comprehend the references to the fairy tales but there were terms that seemed to be used as metaphors in the story. Steedman uses these literary techniques to explain her story, but without having read the other books, I do not know what she is trying to bring across to the readers."

If only I knew the meaning of that word. If only I were familiar with the work to which he or she refers. These are the kinds of issues confronting the readers of texts in which other works are cited. Of course, knowing the meaning of each word and being familiar with all the works a writer cites might make things easier for a reader. But this is neither automatic nor necessary. Neither is it sufficient. You might remember that what helped Connelly enter the landscape of the book was not the straightforward dictionary definition of the term, but the use to which she put it. You might also remember that Connelly herself, when she comes to terms with the fact that as a reader of Steedman's text she must put its bits and pieces together, refers to a work that she and her classmates had read before, *The Dig*. The point is not whether or not you understand better what she says because of that reference. The more intriguing, interesting work for a reader of texts that explicitly refer to others, and even quote them, is to try to understand why a writer might want to make such a move. In Connelly's case, the move reminds her that she already did similar work—and quite well. And she gains support having made that connection. So, when like Connelly, you are stymied by references to works you have not read, rather than expect those other texts to hold the key to your understanding, try to make your understanding of what the need for the connection might reveal be that key.

Here is how Connelly managed this particular difficulty:

> In the section of Carolyn Kay Steedman's *Landscape for a Good Woman,* titled "The Thin Man," I found very few difficulties.
>
> I am beginning to see connections . . . [and] a strong resemblance between Lynn Emanuel's *The Dig* and Steedman's work. I am gaining a new understanding of prose, as I did of poetry. I see both of these works as more of an art of words and literary techniques. They are used in such a way that the author can say things to the audience without specifically naming every detail. At first I found difficulty understanding what the reference to the fairy tale, "The Little Mermaid," had to do with her story. As I read on, I began to see the connection, but I still do not fully understand the meaning. [Finally], on page 55 it becomes clear that the persona represented in the story felt like the mermaid in the other story. She felt as though she wanted to be more than her social class suggested. This is a reference to her mother's feelings as well as her own. She wanted to go above the sea, to the land of opportunity, to see things she never saw and have things she never had.

The kind of process Connelly so successfully initiates and sustains has enabled her to constitute Steedman's book as a landscape, a surveyable territory. Her reading process—transforming the implicit into the explicit and then transforming the explicit in terms of what the implicit has made visible—resonates with a theory about reading by Wolfgang Iser (whom we already mentioned in the Introduction). Iser explains that any text "contains" blanks the reader must fill in. As he puts it, ". . . blanks trigger off and simultaneously control the reader's activity. Blanks indicate that the different segments and patterns of the text are to be connected *even though the text itself does not say so*" (our emphasis) (*The Norton Anthology*, 1677).

But how do we read what is not there? How the connections the perceived gaps call for are established depends very much on what readers bring to the task of reading—their prejudgments, their pre-understandings.

None of us is a *tabula rasa* (blank slate)—we were not born as such and we never are, even when we approach a completely new task, which in our case is the task of reading. Even when we call ourselves "beginners," there is always some kind of knowledge we bring to an unfamiliar task that we instinctively rely on. That is, regardless of how impenetrable a text may at first appear, there is always something in it we can recognize; there is always something we can work with.

What is important is that we become able to identify and use our pre-understandings as a *scaffold* to construct new understandings. As we build upon the scaffold of what we know, our initial knowledge will inevitably change. If we do not build upon what we already know, what we know will remain just that—what we already know: useful, worthwhile, but not necessarily sufficient or adequate to help us move to new situations and in new contexts. Does what I know help me understand this new text? If not, why not? What am I assuming this text should do? What else might this text want to do, want me to do? These are some of the questions you might want to learn to ask as you read texts that seem to surprise you or keep you in check.

Before we move to the next section, we would like for you to flesh out your answers to these questions by revisiting Connelly's work and identifying moments when you see her reading in a way she could not have, had she continued to rely on her initial definition of prose. Had she done that, what would she not have understood?

5

The Difficulty of Prose Narrative

Reading means approaching something that is just coming into being.

—Italo Calvino, *If on a winter's night a traveler*

Narratives: "stories about a series of events, usually in sequence and often with one event causing the other. . . . The content of a narrative is a collection of represented events, along with the participants in those events, and the circumstances of those events. The form of the narrative is the way in which those events are represented through a particular narrative medium. . . . Many components of a narrative show a tension between content and form. . . . A mismatch between form, order and content is an example of an **aesthetic strategy** . . .

—Martin Montgomery, Ann Durant, Nigel Fabb, Tom Furniss, and Sara Mills, *Ways of Reading: Advanced Reading Skills for Students of English Literature*

In the previous chapter—our "Intermezzo"—we made the transition from poetry to prose. In this new chapter, we will build on those ideas about prose, but we will also return to and complicate the discussion about narrative we initiated in Chapter 4. The two epigraphs should give you a sense of our plan:

- To examine in more detail how readers of narrative learn to mine, transfer, and adapt prior knowledge and understanding to a new context (a process referred to by educators as deep learning)
- To examine in more detail how readers (can) scaffold the understanding of narrative they already have to produce strong readings of difficult, demanding, surprising texts
- To make the transition from poetic narrative to prose narrative

As in prior chapters, we will move back and forth between identification and analysis of difficulties, and the creative adjustments they call for.

What You Already Know About Narrative

Let us return for a moment to *The Ancyent Marinere*, and to four responses made by Eileen Tehan. We want to consider how and when a reader's pre-understanding either promotes or limits further understanding:

> The strange ship approaches the Mariner and his crewmembers, who are now desperate for help. As the ship grows closer in distance, the sun begins to set and the atmosphere of the poem becomes dark and gloomy. Could this be foreshadowing future events? I also notice that in stanzas six and seven the "sun" receives a lot of attention . . . What is the importance of the sun in this part of the poem?
>
> This is an important stanza because you would think that the Mariner would be happy to see the arriving ship. Instead the Mariner acts as if it is an intrusion. Why does the Mariner react in this way, and why does he call the ship a strange shape? This indicates to me that something bad is going to happen. The Mariner's dull reaction and his dismal description reinforce my feeling that the ship is not there to help the Mariner and his crewmembers.
>
> I am unsure though whether or not this affects the plot of the poem. This brings up one of the biggest difficulties I had throughout

my analysis of the poem. It is whether or not structure directly affects the plot. Does Coleridge make specific structural choices to enhance his ideas in the poem, or are these choices more a matter of convention? Furthermore if these conventional choices are significant then which ones are and which ones aren't? This has been extremely problematic for me probably even more so than understanding the plot.

Tehan brings to the *Marinere* a viable pre-understanding of narrative, one that she, like so many college students, has formed through years of exposure, in school and other contexts, to the rich and varied practices of stories and storytelling. Some of her comments seem especially important:

- Is there or is there not "foreshadowing"? If so, what use does she make of it as a reader?
- Why does the Mariner respond to the arrival of the strange ship as if it were an intrusion? Why would a reader even pose this question about the *Marinere?*
- What kind of relationship should exist or does exist between structure and plot?

These kinds of questions, and even these terms (once you get over the idea that they are applicable only to literary texts), are probably ones you have heard before and have probably used yourself. As we mentioned in Chapter 3, stories are familiar things. We tell stories, we are told stories, we find stories everywhere. We use stories to structure and convey understanding, to make sense of experience, to turn chaos into order. In the questions she posed, Tehan draws upon her prior understanding, one that is commonsensical but also technical/literary: thus her reference to such specialized terms as foreshadowing, structure, and plot. These terms belong to and encourage us to reflect on a category broader than story—**narrative.**

How Narrative Can Be Theorized: Gerard Genette

Many theories of narrative exist, providing often competing notions of what narratives consist of, what they are designed to do, how they function. We focus on only one here, that provided by Gerard Genette, because it has proven especially helpful in our work with student readers.

From Genette's perspective, a narrative can be understood as having three components: **story, text,** and **narration.** Of these, only the text—the verbal representation of events in speech or writing, the spoken or written discourse itself—is directly available to readers. (Genette's definition of "text" is different than that used earlier in this book. See the Glossary.) The text is what is read. In contrast, the story is something that readers piece together by abstracting events and participants from the text and then arranging what they have selected in accordance with chronological order. (Story and narrative can be identical.) The last term, "narration," represents the filter through which events and participants are presented.

To summarize, we can say that when most readers first read a narrative they usually just pass their eyes across the words, from first page to last. On a second or third reading, through acts of re-imagining and responding to textual cues, they begin to arrange events in temporal order so as to create a story. At every stage, at some level, readers are aware that setting, actions, and characters are being filtered through a narrator's perspective, through a consciousness that is not their own.

Using Theory to Reframe Your Understanding

While you may not have thought about narratives as being analyzable in the way indicated above, it is likely that these terms merely rename functions or characteristics you already are familiar with, if only tacitly. Look again at what Tehan wrote.

In speaking of "foreshadowing" she seems to be thinking about the chronological relationship between events, how one is temporally related to another, and what is to be expected when they are out of synch. But she also seems to be thinking in terms of causality: Why has the Mariner reacted as he has? In speaking of structure and plot, she seems to be envisioning the work she believes that as a reader she is expected to do: to relate events as narrated to those arranged in chronological sequence. If you remember your work with the *Marinere*, you know that the succession of events in the story is indeed different from that in the text. The text begins with the wild-eyed Mariner compelling a poor wedding guest to listen to his story. The story of the Mariner, however, begins with his setting off to sea; his act of narration is the last element in the story, although the first in the text.

This work of reconstruction that the *Marinere*, a narrative poem, requires is work that is triggered and sustained by a reader's understanding of how narratives generally operate. And it is not an easy task. It is work that largely transforms and integrates. Through this work, readers rearrange **events** to create chronological and causal patterns that make sense to them. They ask: What happens next? Why did it happen? Who made it happen? The expectation that events relate to each other in important ways, that events require participants, that events are focalized for us by a narrator, that events are narrated—these expectations shape the reading of narratives and the difficulties readers encounter when reading them.

When they read prose narratives, readers are carried along, in a sense, in ways that are different from when they read poetry, or even poetic narratives. (Notice, however, that being carried along is never passive, and that understanding of previously obscure elements does not happen just through repeated readings.) Narratives can produce an overpowering sense of momentum and trajectory from a beginning, through a middle, and to an end. The movement of narrative is "obvious," like the "flow" of an ordinary sentence is obvious. Both prescribe a linear process: The reader's understanding is controlled to some degree by how certain things are positioned. When reading a narrative, just like when reading a sentence, a reader begins from the very beginning to form a hypothesis (**hypothesis formation**) and to integrate new information, to see how what follows fits or does not fit. If what follows fits, then the hypothesis is sustained; if what follows does not fit, if there is a mismatch, then the hypothesis must change. Or the hypothesis might still fit, but certain conclusions, interpretations, and understandings might have to be modified or replaced.

Think of Tehan again. At first she thought the Mariner would obviously view the sight of an approaching ship with relief—obviously, given her understanding of the circumstances in which he has been placed and how people can generally be expected to respond to such situations. But yet the narrative undermines these expectations. It surprises her. And she initially assumes that surprise to be a difficulty, given certain ideas about continuity she seems to have brought along. But that difficulty can also be looked at as a seductive, enticing moment; It hooks her; it keeps her reading, thinking, examining, testing.

One of the ways narrative hooks us is by withholding information. Gaps in information can orient us to the future ("what's next") or the past ("what happened" or "who did it"). These gaps may be temporary (new information will fill them in) or permanent (they remain open, even after the story ends). But they also hook us by setting up predictable as well as unpredictable patterns. When some readers figure out what narratives are doing early in the game, they may very likely suffer a fateful attack of boredom that will lead them to close the pages. These are readers who expect narratives to keep them surprised, or in a state of suspension, of anticipation. They like it when authors delay the imparting of information. When this does not happen, they feel let down. They find the text difficult to read. But there are also readers who have a special taste for predictability. They like to be led to guess right. When they encounter unexpected turns of events, they are confused. They find the text difficult to read. Although each type of reader may at first be confused by a text that does not fulfill his or her expectations, and experience difficulties, these difficulties are also devices by which each type of narrative keeps itself alive.

Reading *Krik? Krak!*

We want to look at unusual kinds of prose narratives in this chapter, ones that challenge understanding in unpredictable ways. Our decision is strategic. The work we have already done on narrative up to this point is work you can easily duplicate with material that is obviously "imaginary," such as the short story.

In this section we will work with several examples of students' responding to their reading *of Krik? Krak!* by Edwidge Danticat. Danticat was born in Haiti in 1969. She came to the United States when she was 12. At 14, she published her first writing in English. She completed her education in this country, studying and earning a degree in French Literature and an MFA (a degree in creative writing). She is now a well-established writer and has won several prestigious awards.

Krik? Krak! is a collection of stories about the hardships of life in Haiti. Immediately in that statement we identify what makes this text rather unusual: It talks about so-called "real life," but it does so in fictional form. It raises and capitalizes on the issue of what separates fact from **fiction.** This blurring of genres, for which there are no explicit rules, presents as difficult a reading challenge as that presented by Linda Barry's "autobiofictionalography." Furthermore, the text presents a view of Haiti quite different from the glamorized version that used to be prevalent in travel brochures, with its swaying palm trees, pristine beaches, and tourists in sunglasses. Instead, it offers us images such as the following:

> My Madonna cried. A miniature teardrop traveled down her white porcelain face, like dew on the tip of early morning grass. When I saw the tear I thought, surely, that my mother had died.
>
> I sat motionless observing the Madonna the whole day. It did not shed another tear. I remained in the rocking chair until it was night fall, my bones aching from the thought of another trip to the prison in Port-au-Prince. But, of course, I had to go.
>
> The roads to the city were covered with sharp pebbles only half buried in the thick dust. I chose to go barefoot, as my mother had always done on her visits to the Massacre River, the river separating Haiti from the Spanish-speaking country that she had never allowed me to name because I had been born on the night that El Generalissimo, Dios Trujillo, the honorable chief of state, had ordered the massacre of all Haitians living there.
>
> The sun was just rising when I got to the capital. The first city person I saw was an old woman carrying a jar full of leeches. Her gaze was glued to the Madonna tucked under my arm.
>
> "May I see it?" she asked.
>
> I held out the small statue that had been owned by my family ever since it was given to my great-great-great-grandmother Défilé by a French man who had kept her as a slave. (33–34)

An overwhelming difficulty for many of our students at first was the strangeness of this text: What is this place? What kind of world does it represent? But as they tried to come to terms with it, some students moved from vague response ("it is strange") to naming two specific aspects of the text they thought could trigger that response. First, the sections (the chapters) seemed disconnected, a feature that continuously thwarted their attempt to read the text as a "novel." Second, the text's subject matter and specific events seemed overly harsh, unbelievable, and foreign, and hence difficult to understand. In other words, their difficulties had to do both with how the text represents various events and what those events actually are. (Are they credible, believable, real?) In one case, we provide student Julian Betkowski's writing in two successive stages. In the first, the Difficulty Paper stage, we see him mapping out some of the difficulties he encountered reading *Krik? Krak!* In the second, we see him return to those difficulties in a more formal essay, and unfold those difficulties into an analysis of symbols.

We have reproduced below various responses to this text provided by our students. We are going to ask you to work with them closely, and, as you read them, to undertake three different kinds of work. First, we ask you to reflect on the following issues:

- How different readers may filter the same text—through personal associations, emotions, shared background knowledge, and with different outcomes
- How a story is similar to but also different from an historical account of the same event

The second piece of work we invite you to do is construct a repertoire of these writers' reading strategies, returning to the form of the Triple-Entry Notebook:

- In the first column, jot down sentences and phrases that represent interesting or perplexing responses.
- In the second column, consider how the writers' pre-understanding of how to read narratives functions as a scaffold for their reading.
- In the third column, assess how they articulate and test their hypotheses.

Then, based on these ideas you have generated, write a two-page reflective paper on the work that each writer's reading strategies make possible, adapting as you deem appropriate, the instructions given by Professor Falbo to her students (see Chapter 3).

I.

"Are you okay? You've been shot in the head . . . And I'm holding your brains—The old lady said. So I drink in the shadows of an evening sky. See nothing at all." So go the lyrics of *Seven Years in Tibet* by David Bowie. This song leapt instantly to mind while I was reading "Night Women" not so much because of the actual meaning, but because of the tone, sentiment and feeling. As "Night Women" opens, the tone is calm, almost banal, but as the story unfolds the truth slowly reveals its hideous self. Just as David Bowie sings *Seven Years in Tibet* with a cool, withdrawn voice, so does the mother speak unemotionally about her life; it is a harsh counterpoint to the actual meaning of the words. Also present is a feeling of hopelessness. Not only have these horrible events taken place, but now there is no way back; the road to happiness barred forever. Especially poignant, though, is the mother's desire for her son to "see nothing at all." Despite her own problems, her son must not know of her suffering, of what she must do to preserve him. She gives herself to keep him alive and yet refuses to reveal the nature of her livelihood. This is, perhaps, her ultimate sacrifice—she must suffer alone.

Marie knew the child was dead from the moment she picked it up; it must have been cold and it definitely didn't move. Yet she kept it. That initial emotion of motherhood, which swept over her when she first saw Rose, overrode her good sense. She even commented on the idea that it was something which was no longer of any use to anybody. She knew of the danger of her act, but proceeded anyway. I was, at first, curious when there was no mention of feeding the child, so the final revelation was not that surprising. This is the second time that a dead baby has appeared and so it is almost certainly symbolic. Maybe it is a symbol of broken promises: a promise of new life taken away too soon, a promise of love and marriage destroyed by lust, a promise of hope when none can be expected. Celliane's baby had no hope; neither did the boat. (Julian Betkowski)

II.

I can see many difficulties that would arise from most readers in our situation. Most native Americans do not know what it is to live in terror of their life from the authority or even the blind fear of guns. These stories reminded me of Liberia, especially "Children of the Sea." I have a few friends from that country whose families were obliterated during their twelve-year civil war. Their faces were scarred, and one man had lost his arm. He was eleven at the time. This kind of unqualified brutality let me see the author's images with a clarity that was chilling. However, for all of that grief and sadness, my friends could always make me laugh with their stories and gossip about their home village. Their stories and songs seemed to sustain them through all of their bad memories and made them stronger, just like the people on the boat out of Haiti in "Children of the Sea." I sometimes wish that I had the same connection with folklore or song that those people did, because we all need to draw strength at times.

However, trying to think through the personal problems of the characters always gives me more of a difficulty than the larger and more obvious problem of a character's cause or country. They are always more fragile and complicated. In "Children of the Sea," the daughter's relationship with her father is tragic but in a way beautiful towards the end, when the father showed as much emotion as it seemed he was capable of. His hand on her shoulder brought the news of her love's death. Her mother's prophecy of a choice between her father and her love proved true, and her hope seemed to die when the news of the boat came to her, just like hope died when the old president failed to return. It always seemed to me that love and hope were synonymous, but for this woman, love continued even though hope was gone. (Michael Mastroianni)

III.

Krik? Krak! was a fairly easy read with highly interesting and intense subject matter; however, I did encounter two main difficulties. The first problem I encountered with the subject of genre. I was expecting it to be a novel; however, the genre appeared to be a compilation of short stories . . . The second, and far more interesting, difficulty I encountered [was] with subject matter . . . I often found myself shocked . . . that people lived such lives and managed to survive (physically, emotionally, and mentally). The story "Night Women" contained particularly difficult subject matter . . . I usually do not think of a prostitute as a caring mother who is forced into that life style to support herself and her family, so it forced me to think beyond the stereotypes I had created for prostitutes . . . I often found myself searching and hoping for a story that would have a "happy" ending, because it [is] hard for me to accept that there were no "happy" endings . . . When reading any material, even difficult material, I have an expectation that at least I will leave the text feeling there is hope.

Another difficulty I had was in understanding the ending of each story. In some stories, such as the first, the dualism is left unresolved (note: the writer views the book's title as suggesting duality: first "Krik," then "Krak"); the two stories do not come together. In others, however, Danticat resolves the dualism in the end . . . An example would be the second story, when the daughter's feelings merge with those of her fallen mother, when she joins her struggle to fly. Was I supposed to look for a resolution to the dualism in the story, or was the point of Danticat's writing to emphasize how the hellish situations in Haiti create dualisms that cannot be resolved? This leads me to my final difficulty . . . My plan for unity was disrupted. (Heather Bastian)

Understanding Strange Texts

While we are hesitant to say much about these three texts—since we have invited you to explore them for yourself—a few comments might be useful in setting up the rest of our discussion. We said that most students commented on the strangeness of *Krik? Krak!* The Difficulty Papers we have introduced show two specific strategies to deal with it: Writers either attempt to circumvent the strangeness of the text by establishing its familiarity (through a song, through the experiences of friends and family) or they attempt to focalize it by pointing to its deviation from what they consider the law of genre (stories should be unified, endings happy, themes resolved).

- Describe how, and with what effects, these writers tested some of their hypotheses.
- Describe what they were able to do by using two terms culled from their encounter with other genres.
- Describe, especially in the examples of the last two writers, the important new work that their identification of what they did *not* understand led them to generate.

Then, develop the observation you have gathered in response to these prompts, and what you wrote in the two-page reflective paper, into notes for a four-page essay that you will write when you have completed your work with this chapter. Title it "On Reading Difficult Texts." Model it on Montaigne's essay (see Chapter 7).

You might have noticed that these student readers sometimes allude to but never directly write about the difficulty of confronting frightening and ugly representations of existence. Such a difficulty is often mentioned in classroom discussions about texts like *Krik! Krak?* and other works that create vivid impressions of horrific experiences (think for a moment about Holocaust literature). In this case, the work is difficult more for what it says than how it says (although, obviously, that distinction is artificial, since it is the "how" that creates the sense of vividness and engagement). It is its sense of authenticity, of historicity, that contributes to its power. Readers understand that at one level they are encountering the "real." Thus, Heather Bastian addresses how she wanted a "happy ending," but she understands that in this instance her desire would not be satisfied, for the experiences being written about were real, not imagined. That brings us to a consideration of terms that for many readers of fiction establish a significant and highly problematic distinction—that between truth and fiction.

Reading the "Story" in "History"

The conflict between truth and fiction strikes many as simply a matter of common sense, although that difference remains a philosophical conundrum. And narrative plays a role in calling this conflict into question. You may want to return to the discussion of *Krik? Krak!* by our student writers to try to identify at what points they seem to be talking about "truth" or "fiction."

Having identified those moments, let us rewrite the conflict between "truth" and "fiction" in terms of another **binary opposition**—that between history and story—since it is often to history we turn to learn about "real-life" situations like those represented in *Krik? Krak!* We offer a quotation and a suggestive etymological description to stimulate or sharpen your response:

- What's real and what's true aren't necessarily the same (Salman Rushdie, *Midnight's Children*, 189).

- Both "story" and "history" derive from the Greek *historia,* "learning by inquiry," and from *histor,* "a person who knows or sees." In its origin, therefore, story implies a way of knowing. The word "narrative" comes from the Latin *narrare/narratum,* "to tell or narrate." And it is ultimately derived from the archaic word *gnarus* which meant "knowing," a word which is also the source of the word "cognition." (adapted from *Literature* by Peter Widdowson, 133–34).

What these questions and relationships suggest is that the difference between truth and fiction is not as simple or as clear cut as we may wish. What makes it difficult to differentiate them?

The interdependence of these categories and their mutual implication gives rise to some significant considerations. That is, is it possible that we generalize to all narratives models of patterning, ordering, and sequencing that are specific to imaginative texts? Heather Bastian expects "happy endings." Why? The reason may be that she has assimilated from various contemporary sources (other books, television programs, etc.) narrative patterns found in early romances (another literary genre), in which a hero sets out on a quest, confronts challenges, wins his heart's desire. When people talk about each generation of Americans being more successful than the previous one, are they not referring implicitly, and unconsciously, to the narrative of progress? Because such narratives entail a vision of the world in its grandest metaphysical terms, they are called **grand** (or master) **narratives.** Such narratives are reassuring. They give us confidence.

Think about historical narrative for a moment. Do writers of history consider issues of arrangement, selection, and focalization? Can attention to these issues affect the representation of historic truths? Keep these ideas in mind when, in a few sections, we consider the personal narrative—the story about selfhood we create for others, and ourselves.

Understanding the Language of Prose

We now turn to another level of difficulty our student readers registered: that which occurs when prose acts in unpredictable ways, when it "sounds" not like prose or "ordinary language" at all but like *poetry.* In other words, what difficulty results when the language of prose appears to deviate from what is thought to be a standard—in this case, the "standard" of "prosaic" language? (Go back to Chapter 2 and review our discussion of these matters.) In the two following sections we will focus on two of these apparent deviations: tone and symbol.

Tone in Prose

Do you remember how Connelly wrote about "tone" and the way in which it affected, and guided, her response to Steedman's writing? Now, we want to shift your attention to the tone of the four writers we featured. We want you to describe and analyze your response to how and what they write about their reading, and its effect on you as a reader. By the way, if you did notice these moments, or others like them, you were focusing on what these writers were actually saying, because their narratives "hooked" you. What features of their writing grabbed your attention? Make a note of strategies you might productively adapt to your writing needs.

We know that tone is a concept probably most familiar to you in considerations of writing, where it generally is understood to convey the writer's attitude to the subject matter. This very reason makes tone especially relevant to considerations of reading because it signals to you how the writer (and/or narrator) *feels* about what he or she is writing (or representing). Thus, we want you to look at tone as a mediating structure—a writer's way with words that may invite in or keep at a distance his/her reader from the experiences written about.

The writers we introduced earlier are all writing about *Krik?Krak!* But, of course, they are also writing about themselves, insofar as their reading—as it is captured in their writing—may reveal aspects of their personality, what they know, how they think:

- What influences, desires, assumptions, kinds of knowledge do you see at work in these Difficulty Papers?
- How do they shape these students' readings?
- How do they enable these readers/writers to enter this "foreign" landscape of *Krik?Krak!*?
- How do they take you along on their journey?

Symbols in Prose

While readers of poetry expect to find symbols everywhere, it is less likely for readers of prose to expect them. But there are instances of prose replete with symbols, as in the case of *Krik? Krak!* Julian Betkowski mentions the word "symbol" in the excerpt you read. And he does not seem to be surprised by the presence of symbols in this text. The difficulty he experiences has less to do with whether or not symbols belong in prose, than with how a symbol is to be identified and interpreted. What we learn from the work he does is how an expectation of symbolism can either enhance or derail an interpretation. But what is a symbol?

In *The Limits of Interpretation,* Umberto Eco offers a definition of symbols (which he attributes to idealistic philosophy) "as **signifiers** that convey imprecise clouds or nebulae of meaning that they leave continually unexploited or unexploitable." But, he adds, for logicians and mathematicians, a symbol is something much more exact, and precise. It is:

> . . . either a signifier correlated to its meaning by a law, that is, by a precise convention, and as such interpretable by other signifiers, or a variable that can be bound in many ways but that, once it has acquired a given value, cannot represent other values within the same context (8).

Eco traces the ambivalence of "symbol" to its Greek etymology.

> Originally a symbol was a token, the present half of a broken table or coin or medal, that performed its social and semiotic function by recalling the absent half to which it potentially could be reconnected. This potentiality was indeed crucial because, since the two halves could be reconnected, it was unnecessary to yearn for the reconnection (9).

And he argues that "the present half of the broken medal, by evoking the ghost of its absent companion and of the original wholeness, encouraged other senses of 'symbol.'" These other senses, he suggests, are captured by the word *synballein,* which meant "to meet, to try an interpretation, to make a conjecture, to solve a riddle, to infer from something imprecise, because incomplete, something else that it suggested, evoked, revealed, but did not conventionally say" (9).

As you read Julian Betkowski's interpretation of symbols in *Krik? Krak!*, keep in mind the two remarkably different definitions of symbols Eco provides. Consider their different functions and the two remarkably different kinds of reading they call for. Which of the two definitions guides Betkowski's reading? With what results?

Below is the beginning of an essay in which Betkowski revises and expands his initial hypothesis about how symbols work in this text. (See the Appendix for the assignment.)

While reading *Krik? Krak!*, by Edwidge Danticat, I encountered the most difficulties when I attempted to decipher the symbolism; more specifically, the symbolism of the dreams. The main reason for my confusion, I believe, is that most of the patently symbolic passages do not draw on traditional literary sources, but instead rely on ideas or images previously presented within the text in some other form. This makes the unraveling of the symbolism a much more complex task since it is so deeply woven into the fabric of the book. However, since there is so much symbolism present in this novel, I will attempt to focus mainly on the dream segments.

Dreams first appear as a major symbolic device in the story "Night Women." This story is about a woman, who after having a child, was abandoned by her lover. As a result, she must make her living by prostituting herself. Sadly, her house has only one room, and her son must sleep in the bed adjacent to the one in which she performs her duties. As a result, she induces sweet dreams in his head while he sleeps so that he will not be woken by her private business. The symbolism here is relatively simple and is almost explained within the story itself. In justifying her actions, she first says that, "I want him to forget that we live in a place where nothing lasts" (Danticat, 86). She continues later on saying, "I tell him that we are expecting a sweet angel and where angels tread the hosts must be as beautiful as floating hibiscus" (Danticat, 86). It is fairly easy to see that the angel is her client of the night and that she acts only in the best interests of her son. In fact, it seems that she is sacrificing herself so that her son might live, at the very least, a content life. She wants him to forget that the world they live in is so transient that even his father left, fading away into the past. Yet even in this bleak environment, she still tries to instill hope into her young son and, perhaps, the dream that his father will one day return. She even uses the return of his father as a protection, for should he awaken while she is with a client, she will tell him that, " . . . his father has come, that an angel has brought him back from Heaven for a while" (Danticat, 88). Still, she strives only to protect him and distance him from the hopelessness of his world. She attempts to build in him an optimism, that one day everything will resolve into happiness. When he wakes in the night, only to find the angel gone, he asks, "Mommy, have I missed the angels again?" To this she replies, "Darling, the angels themselves have a lifetime to come to us" (Danticat, 88).

In the first paragraph, Betkowski talks about "deciphering" and "unraveling" symbols. Using your own examples, explain the work of reading that deciphering and unraveling entail.

Read the section of the book Betkowski is writing about ("Night Women"). We have included it in the Appendix. Then answer in writing the following questions as fully as you can.

- "The symbolism here is relatively simple," says Betkowski. Is it? Look for moments in his writing where what he claims is so simple does not seem to be so simple at all.
- Mark moments when Betkowski's ease with reading simplifies important textual difficulties.
- Did you start "unraveling" the text at the same place he does? If not, did it make a difference in your reading?
- How did your pre-understanding of angels affect the reading of the scene?
- Revisit Heather Bastian's response to "Night Women." What kind of pre-understandings does she bring to this reading, and how do they frame her response? What does she see in this text that Betkowski does not? And vice versa?

Finally, research the history of Haiti and its relation to the United States. Your teacher will direct you to appropriate sources. This could be an individual or group project. Discuss in class what you learned about Haiti that you could not have guessed from the student responses and the excerpts from *Krik?Krak!*, as well aspects of that history that student responses to *Krik?Krak!* brought to life for you. Then write a four-page essay on what counts as "truth" in history and fiction. Think of a title that might "hook" your audience. Use an epigraph that might guide your reader's interpretation of your text. Check the MLA Style Sheet or the *Chicago Manual of Style* for appropriate conventions.

Taking Stock

At the end of Chapter 1, we asked you to make an inventory of new terms, concepts, and ideas. Take a look at that list. If you understand those terms (or some of them) differently—and you must, given the work you have done so far—how would you describe that change? What caused it?

- Which of the terms you entered in your Triple-Entry Notebook is getting more attention from you? Why? Which of the columns is easier or more difficult to write in? Which is the most crowded?
- What do you understand about the use of this strategy that might have confused you before? What has changed in the moves you make as a reader, writer, and thinker?
- Write two paragraphs of instruction and advice to a student who is now beginning the journey you began at the beginning of this book. What would you want him or her to know? What did we not take into account that we should have?
- Give an example of the kind of "understanding" that the Difficulty Paper and the Triple-Entry Notebook helped you achieve. (This can be used in your advice to the student.)
- Write your own "assisted invitation" for prospective students: a reading assignment that grows out of a reading strategy you have found particularly helpful. (This might be a collaborative exercise.)

Retrospective

This chapter builds on ideas about prose provided in the "Intermezzo." It also returns to the discussion of prose initiated in Chapter 3. Once again, we asked you to begin your work by examining your repertoire, but this time by reviewing the substantial knowledge about narrative you brought to this chapter. You were then encouraged to reframe those pre-understandings in theoretical terms, using a vocabulary provided by Gerard Genette. The chapter then reexamined a student text in terms of that language in order to demonstrate the incipient knowledge you may possess but may not have yet articulated or made visible. Much of this chapter focused on the narrative *Krik! Krak?*, a text that may initially seem strange because it violates expectations about subject consistency and organization. We saw how students, engaging in the process of hypothesis-formation, initially labeled as difficult any part of it that interfered with their process of "meaning-making" (and we also discussed the defamiliarizing effect—a term already introduced—of these surprises). Finally, the chapter concluded with the challenges created when prose violates expectations of an assumed standard.

6

Writing and Reading the Personal Essay

> The personal essay is, in my experience, a form of discovery. What one discovers in writing such essays is where one stands on complex issues, problems, questions, subjects. In writing the essay, one tests one's feelings, instincts, thoughts in the crucible of composition.
>
> —Joseph Epstein, editor, *The Norton Book of Personal Essays*

> Thus, reader, myself am the matter of book.
>
> —Montaigne, *Essais*

The previous chapter examined the difficulties that arise when readers encounter prose narratives. This chapter builds on those ideas, but it also pursues a new direction. Up to this point, we have asked you to access and articulate your tacit knowledge about *reading* and then apply that knowledge to your own *writing*. That is, we have posited that you improve as a writer by becoming a reflexive and engaged reader of difficult texts. And we have urged you to make, rather than assume it as automatic, a transfer of the understanding that reading makes possible to writing.

Now we will ask that you reverse the movement. We will ask you to mine the understanding you think the processes of *writing* make possible and to adapt, revise, or transfer it to *reading*. In this chapter we will ask you to reflect on the work we assume you have already done as a practitioner of the genre called the **personal essay** or narrative. We will ask you to think, in particular, about the issues of selfhood, identity, and ***subjectivity*** that discussions of "the personal" tend to provoke. We will then ask you to reframe your understanding of these issues by examining a personal essay written by Michel de Montaigne. (It is entitled "Of Books" and can be found on the Internet on the Gutenberg Project site at http://onlinebooks.library.upenn.edu/.) We focus on personal writing in this discussion of reading and writing because, of all the genres discussed in this book, it is perhaps the one that makes the convergence between them most perceivable.

Writing About the Self

As our brief comments about historical narratives suggest, all writing is to some degree "personal." That is, it reflects a writer's personal choices and reactions, even when it is coached in "objective" language. When we talk about the personal essay or narrative, however, we are referring more specifically to a type of writing marked by certain features. Such writing may be organized in different ways, conceptually (as in the personal essay) or chronologically (as in the personal narrative). These organizational structures are not mutually exclusive; a single piece of writing may avail itself of both.

Here are some examples of personal writing produced in a first-year writing course at Lafayette College focused on the topic of education.

I remember hating attending piano lessons each week in my teacher's house. She enforced discipline more than my teachers at school had. Although I caught on quickly, memorizing unfamiliar notes, keys, and clefs was tiring. Each week she made sure I played every note correctly or she forced me to start over. She controlled the amount of new information that I would be exposed to and chose the appropriate pieces for my experience level. Paulo Freire would define this method of learning as "banking." In the "banking" scheme of education, a student is forcefully fed lessons without any choice or freedom of the subject matter. "Narration (with the teacher as narrator) leads the students to memorize mechanically the narrated content" (Freire 349). (Sally Amen)

Reading Freire's revolutionary essay about the education system allowed me to put a name to my previously unexplainable problems with the way in which I learn. I am also able to see how some of Freire's statements apply to my current classes and see the "banking" method of education in action. In a particular class of mine, art history, I finally understand how the method of educating that my teacher uses dictates how I will respond to a class and what I will get out of a class. (Nick Baldwin)

Reading Ralph Waldo Emerson taught me that education is found not just in books, but also in all of life's experiences. We cannot rely on any one source—book, teacher, or experience—to learn, and during my first semester, I relied too much on one source myself. We must gather a variety by interacting with people, visiting places around the world, participating in activities, and reading widely. Isolating ourselves is counterproductive for learning. A man must not "Shut [himself] out of his globe of action, and transplant an oak into a flower pot, there to hunger and pine; nor trust the revenue of some single faculty, and exhaust one vein of thought" (Emerson 239). Like Emerson, I now believe there is so much to learn from our world, an infinite amount of truth to fit into the infinite capacity of our minds. (Kevin Chysna)

What characteristics do these reflections have in common? What moves do you see each of the writers making? Why do they shift from personal experience to citation? What makes that move necessary in each example?

If we were to infer the conventions of personal writing from the previous examples, we might say the following:

- It uses "I." And this "I" refers directly to the writer, not to an imaginary character.
- It describes the writer's personal experience or offers personal reflection.

- It creates a bridge between writer and reader by using that experience or reflection as an example of something larger, with the hope that the reader can "relate." In the previous examples, that larger frame of reference is provided through theories of education.

What makes personal writing an especially interesting genre to explore is that its *subject* or topic is actually *the subject.* That is, as can be seen in our brief excerpts, although each writer mentions someone else's ideas, it is his or her reaction to those ideas, or understanding of them, or an ability to use them as interpretive frameworks for experience that is really the focus of the piece. Personal writing, in brief, can be understood as a *story about the self.* Subject, self—these are terms more complex than they may at first seem. To write *about* the self, to take *one's self as one's subject* is an especially difficult task although, at first consideration, it might seem otherwise. After all, whom do we know better than ourselves?

Reflecting on Personal Writing

Given what we know about our educational system, we are confident you have written a personal essay (perhaps even in your application to college), and we are going to ask you to draw upon that experience. At the very least, in this book, you have repeatedly engaged in personal writing, sometimes as random meditations on your reading, sometimes in more structured discussions of difficulty.

Now we ask you to activate your stored knowledge about the personal essay (or narrative—for our purposes here, the two terms can be used interchangeably). First, we ask you to consider the following questions. Second, we ask you once again to write a version of the personal essay called the literacy narrative.

- When did you write a personal essay? In which context or class?
- What goal was such writing to have?
- What directions were you provided? If the directions called for an "essay," what did you think you were expected to do? Did the essay designation invite speculation on your part?

- If it was part of a course work, where was this writing positioned in the course of the semester? Was it the first assignment? If not, what preceded it and what followed it?
- Since this kind of writing is a genre like any other, how would you identify its conventions?
- Would you say your language was "poetic" or "prosaic," and in the context of the personal essay what would these words mean?
- Would you say that this writing was more or less creative than any other course writing you have done? We are especially interested in how you understand the word "creative," one of those code words we referred to in Chapter 1.
- Do you find this kind of writing more or less pleasurable than other kinds? Would you say it is easier, less difficult? Again, as you use these words, remember that what you mean by them might not be immediately evident to others.
- Finally, do you undertake personal writing on your own time, outside of class? If so, in what form: journal, diary, letters, e-mail, instant messenger? Why do you do this kind of writing? When you undertake it for personal reasons, what are your specific goals?

Respond to these questions in any form that feels comfortable to you. But as you answer them, consider what might have been our plan in asking them.

At this point, we ask you to undertake a second, more formal kind of work, the literacy narrative. In this narrative, we ask you to describe as carefully as you can your experiences as a writer, beginning with your earliest memories (remember in Chapter 2 we asked you to undertake a similar kind of work with respect to your history as a reader) and moving to the present context. Think, in particular, of the books you read, their impact on you as a writer, your reasons for remembering them.

Uncovering the Difficulty of Personal Writing

We mentioned a few passages prior that it often seems that personal writing—because its subject is what we assume to know best—would be a relatively easy genre to work with. And before you wrote your literacy narrative, you might have thought so yourself. But what that experience might have suggested to you, as has our work with students over many years, is that the simplicity of the personal essay is deceiving. While some types of writing may seem at first difficult to undertake (at least until you realize that you already possess the tools you need), the literacy narrative may be an example of something that seems easy at first but turns out to be difficult. Simply because something is familiar—as our history as writers would seem to be (and if not to us, then to whom?)—does not mean that it will promote a sense of ease.

Here is a list of questions that aim at uncovering why this kind of writing might indeed prove difficult. With your latest essay in hand, try to re-imagine the actual work of producing it, as you keep the following issues in mind:

- What decisions did you have to make in selecting details and events to write about? What did you exclude, and why?
- What decisions did you have to make in arranging these details and events?
- What decisions did you have to make in deciding which of the details or events to emphasize and which not to emphasize?
- Are there moments in your writing where you tried to create a sense of delay, or suspense, or foreshadowing?
- Turning to the discussion of Genette's narrative theory provided in the previous chapter, examine what you wrote in terms of the categories he provides. In other words, examine it as a narrative, with a narrator, a text, a story.

As your answers to these questions may suggest, it can be difficult to know which criteria to use to select which experiences to write about. How do memory, forgetfulness, and suppression affect a writer's selection?

What about the order of the narrative of one's life? Is conceptual or chronological order the only structuring principle? And here is an idea that we feel confident will strike you at first as strange: Narratives of one's life tend to reproduce narratives of other lives. What does that mean? (Remember Connelly's work with *Landscape?*)

You might want to consider another difficulty of the genre. While we might think that the details of the stories we tell about ourselves are "true," "special" bits of ourselves, the patterns we use to organize those events tend to be borrowed or adapted from what we have read, what we have seen endlessly duplicated in television and movies, what we have been told by other people. Narrative, in particular, is a *form,* and just as poets borrow poetic forms and adapt them for their own purposes, so do writers of narrative. (See our discussion in Chapter 5.) If our self stories are marked by the stories of other selves, how "authentic" or "sincere" or "true" are the tales we tell about ourselves? If even this question is baffling, give some consideration as to why.

Now reread your literacy narrative. What kind of events does it offer? Do they add up to a story dominated by resistances? Obstacles? Successes? What if you rewrote your story to emphasize a different series of events or set of narrative parameters? Would you still think of your story as "truthful"?

Now rewrite your literacy narrative in the form of a poem. Use as a model one of the poems included in this book, but the poem you write should not exceed two pages. Give it a title and an epigraph (look at how we have used epigraphs and what function we have given them). Use title and epigraph as clues for your readers. Then write a reflexive commentary in which you describe the goals you had, your intention, the choice of form you made and why, and how that choice affected the story you told in poetic form. What was especially difficult about writing your life in verse (even in **free verse**)? Which of your difficulties were enabling? Which were real obstacles? How did you solve them?

We are suggesting here that even stories of the self—which we often assume we intimately know—may uncover *contradictions* of the self. They may display a self in *transition.* Or a self that does not understand itself (and so a reader may see more than a writer does). Or a self that changes from moment to moment.

Thus, we are also suggesting here that the self that is, after all, the subject of such stories, may not be stable or coherent or fully available to the writer. It may not be so familiar, after all. A self changes, depending on situation, context, and the others who surround it. And that is not to be taken as a sign of dysfunction or ethical unreliability, but of the complexity of *identity* itself. Think about it. Is your "student self" the same as your "romantic self" or your "family self" or your "athlete self"? Are you the same person at this moment as you were when you began this book? As you were in high school? As you will be tomorrow? A week later? Perhaps all that can be confidently said about the self—

yours, ours—is that it is fundamentally unstable. It is transient, malleable, protean, plastic, revisionary. If it weren't, how dull and predictable life would be! Let us work on these ideas by reflecting on Montaigne's essay and a student reader's response to it.

Exploring the Self: The Example of Montaigne

Michel Montaigne is a sixteenth-century writer who is widely credited with having created the form of the essay as a prose *exploration* of the self. (If the idea of the self as something to *explore* sounds odd, why is this the case? Would some other verb be more suitable?) For Montaigne, the word "essai" meant a trial, a test. (Does knowing this about Montaigne change in any way the way you read him?) Drawing from the pioneering writing of Montaigne, we could then add the following item to the characteristics of personal writing presented earlier: A personal essay places the self under trial, puts it to the test.

By suggesting that personal writing puts it to the test, we do not mean that there is a set of fixed rules by which it can be measured. The kind of test we are referring to is something more fundamental, but also ephemeral, immaterial. It is an exploration of who one is, of what it means to be a self. It is a "quest of knowledge." In Montaigne's case, that quest unfolds as he reflects on the kind of *reader* he is and as he undertakes that reflection in *writing*.

Montaigne is aware that we tend to think of ourselves as individuals, as unique beings. But the major vehicle we have for presenting our unique self is language, and language is common to others and bound to conventions. (Earlier we spoke about contradictory selves.) Language is not something we create. We learn it. We acquire it. And others learn and acquire it in very similar ways. Given that fact, what does it mean to say "I am"? Is this "self" we write and talk about one that is authentic and really unique? (As we raise these questions, we are not suggesting that human beings are inherently inauthentic and common.)

Reading "Of Books"

As you shall see shortly, reading books leads Montaigne to pose questions that touch upon issues of existence, of life. But they are also very specifically questions about reading and writing, and the kind of thinking a self does *while* reading and writing. Montaigne the reader asks: What am I thinking? Why do I think it? Why did I think this was important? How is it meaningful to me now? Montaigne the writer *rewrites* the texts he has read in order to establish their importance to him *personally*. But insofar as it is *his* self that asks these questions, that self changes and expands. The "I" that Montaigne creates is always subject to revision, always under construction, always in process.

Turn now to your copy of the essay "Of Books." As you read it, use whatever system of notation you have been developing as you work with this book (see Chapter 1). At the very least, consider the ideas about autobiography you bring to this essay and the ways in which Montaigne's essay illustrates, confirms, or challenges them. As you read, circle words and phrases that are especially dense.

- What are those moments you find especially difficult or disorienting? Why?
- Would additional information help your understanding? If not, what would? What might you need to do?
- Locate those places where Montaigne sets himself in opposition to **commonsense** ideas, or seems to contradict himself. What might his purpose be?
- Locate examples of poetic language. What function do they serve? What is their effect on you?
- Is Montaigne always in control of his discourse? If not, where does he seem to lose control? What makes you notice that? Why?

Now return to this essay and pay attention to how Montaigne constructs himself as a reader. Drawing upon the work you as reader have done in this book, what would you say about his reading?

- What does he read? What kinds of books does he find important and why?
- Locate moments where he engages in hypothesis formation.
- How does he identify and classify his difficulties? How does he negotiate them?
- Would it be fair to say that Montaigne's sense of who he is is very much related to what and how he reads? If so, who exactly is Montaigne?

Reading Against the Grain

Here are some comments on Montaigne by Richard Regosin, whose name should by now be familiar to you. Some of his words may be especially difficult for you. Such theory talk is often challenging. But remember that you need not understand everything he says in order to understand the gist of it.

> But the hybrid figure of the *Essais* discloses the many faces of textuality, the complex nature of its internal contradictions, its competing inclinations to truth and dissimulation, to faithfulness and betrayal, to form and to deformation.
>
> The essayist himself at times encourages readers to read against the grain by his restless questioning of his own writing and his interrogation of the nature and status of his book, but the reader must also take into account what the text expresses obliquely and what it often discloses in spite of itself, paying particular attention to its unexamined assumptions and implications.

We want you to work closely with these two paragraphs. If they are difficult, is their difficulty a matter of vocabulary? Circle the words whose meaning you do not know. Check them in a dictionary. Does knowing what they mean make the passages less difficult to understand? If the difficulty is not only a matter of vocabulary, how would you define it?

Think about the phrases/metaphors Regosin uses to describe writing and reading. What does "reading against the grain" mean? How does a reader know when he can or must read "against the grain"? What are some of the clues Regosin gives you?

Some of the terms Regosin uses to highlight the richness of Montaigne's writing, "the many faces of textuality," might perplex you: "contradictions," "dissimulation," "betrayal," "deformation." What makes you sense that he is *not* using them to indict the author? How many ways of reading does Regosin claim Montaigne's text activates? And how does a reader negotiate them? Who performs these readings? Finally, do Regosin's comments resonate with your own experience with Montaigne? Does he enable you to better identify and understand your difficulties? Keep an accurate record of your answers to these questions, and keep them in mind as we move to the next section.

Writing About Montaigne: Tom Brennan

Here is a paper by Tom Brennan, a student who was asked to reflect on an earlier Difficulty Paper he wrote in response to "Of Books." In this piece of writing, Brennan returns to work he did in the first weeks of the semester and rewrites it in light of later work (this is a first-year writing course, emphasizing autobiography).

As you have certainly already noted, the kind of essay that Montaigne himself wrote does not conform to the conventions generally taught in college writing courses; his work is not "clear," "direct," "argumentative." It is not thesis-driven, nor are its paragraphs organized around a single idea. He changes his mind, reflects on often contradictory perspectives, and acknowledges and demonstrates the influence of other people's ideas and opinions on his own. His essays are openly intertextual. And they are more exploratory than expository.

Here is Tom Brennan's essay. To what extent is it also *intertextual*, a hybrid? How do you know when Brennan is revising or confirming former opinions? What did he revise? What do those revisions teach us about what he has learned?

Even after reading "Of Books" through the second time, I still found Michel Montaigne to contradict himself. For example, Montaigne writes an opinion paper that discusses the effect that books have on his life. Through his quest of writing Montaigne critiques other authors. The contradiction occurs when Montaigne asks the reader not to hold him, as the writer, responsible for his work.

> This is purely the essay of my natural facilities, and not at all of the acquired ones; and whoever shall catch me in ignorance will do nothing against me, for I should hardly be answerable for my ideas to others, I who am not answerable for them to myself, or satisfied with them.

This inconsistency did not make the paper technically difficult; however, it did add a flavor to the writing that didn't lend itself to my taste. When Montaigne tells me that if I find a mistake within the writing or when I disagree with one of his opinions, this flaw is not his fault; it appears that he does not want to take responsibility for his own writing. This alone seems to be a contradiction. Montaigne writes an essay trying to "find himself" yet is ashamed of his opinions: "And so the opinion I give of them is to declare the measure of my sight, not the measure of things."

From this, I drew the conclusion that Montaigne may be ashamed of himself and thus adds to the multitude of apologies throughout the essay. Why would Montaigne write an essay that is full of criticism toward other writers and still ask that we, the readers, be lenient with the criticisms toward his writing. I find it hard to offer this sympathy.

In the original essay I wrote that on page 47 Montaigne offers a loose interpretation of "them."

> Knowledge and truth can lodge in us without judgment, and judgment also without them; Indeed the recognition of ignorance is one of the fairest and surest testimonies of judgment that I find.

After rereading this passage I now believe that Montaigne is referring to both knowledge and truth. I found that when I read the first time I was focused on the idea of analyzing the work and thus missed a literal meaning. Knowledge and truth can occur without judgment, and therefore judgment without them . . .

I found that Montaigne indeed has a style. After trying to write my paper based on Montaigne, I found the illusion of thinking very difficult to reproduce on paper. Montaigne does this very well. The descriptions stimulate his memory.

Often Montaigne uses vivid generalizations . . . As I went back over the essay after spending a few weeks away, I found I knew the content . . .

At the beginning of the semester I did not enjoy Montaigne's style, nor did I believe that he had one. As I reread the essay, it is actually more calculated and interesting than I had originally believed. Now that I am not struggling . . . I am open to the little bits of humor that are cleverly inserted into the text.

As Brennan explains, he encountered several kinds of difficulties in his first reading of Montaigne's essay. Some of them disappeared after rereading. Some did not. For example, Brennan still sees Montaigne as contradicting himself, saying one thing, only to undercut it; criticizing someone else's writing, only to implore us to ignore his flaws. Why does the word "contradiction" function as an indictment in Brennan's writing, but not in Regosin's?

Although the difficulties he experiences do not bring Brennan's reading to a stop, they do "add a flavor to the writing that didn't lend itself to my taste." They suggest to him that while Montaigne does "not want to take responsibility," he is "ashamed of himself," but Brennan is unwilling "to offer this sympathy." Brennan then refers to a prior difficulty that he was able to resolve—a confusing pronoun reference that he now reads in two ways; earlier Brennan had missed the "literal meaning."

The final issue for Brennan is style, which leads us to say a few words about the context for Brennan's essay. It actually represents the second essay he wrote on Montaigne; the first was a stylistic imitation, in response to the following assignment:

> Assignment: Choosing any subject you would like to reflect on or offer an exploration of (perhaps because of your *pre-understanding?*) write an essay that could, in a sense, have been written by Montaigne. That is, it should be an essay whose goal is conceptual exploration, *revision.* Your writing should circle around the subject, view it from several (even contradictory) perspectives, consider it in isolation and in relationship with other subjects. Since you are imitating Montaigne, you need also to cite from several texts, to react to them: how they have become part of you, or how you have positioned yourself in opposition to them, and so on. While by the end of the essay you will have demonstrated the complexity of your subject, you should aim for something more. For, finally, it is your self which is the "subject" of this essay. That self is one which has changed as the result of your reading and testing of ideas.

In a version of the essay presented earlier, Brennan mentioned that he found this imitation essay difficult to execute because the idea that writing could *enact* rather than simply *reflect* or *copy* a way of thinking was bizarre (a not unusual reaction when "common sense" is challenged). In the later version, the one we presented earlier, his idea about this concept has acquired subtlety. That is, he now understands Montaigne as having made *choices* that, in turn, have consequences. He can now offer an explanation as to why, for example, Montaigne cites others' work so freely: Montaigne is trying to stimulate his own memory, fire up his own engines.

And Brennan now seems to understand that the difficulties he had experienced when first reading Montaigne resulted from his assumptions (pre-understandings) about non-fictional prose, the essay, academic writing. For example, he had assumed that prose should be unified, and that if it is not, it is contradictory. He had assumed that writers should demonstrate their sincerity by maintaining an impersonal distance, by ignoring the presence of their readers. That distance lends objectivity to their writing. It makes readers trust their writing.

At this time, we ask you to read Montaigne's essay once more, this time through Brennan's eyes. Think about style and strategy. If you understand Montaigne as presenting a mind engaged in the *reading process*, are his "contradictions" more or less problematic? Give some thought as to how you use this word "contradiction." Think of another word that might help you to understand, and to express, what Montaigne is doing in a different way.

Making the Move to the Academic Essay

We now ask you to take a final step. While this chapter has emphasized the genre of personal writing (although as we have already said, there is an argument to be made for a personal subtext in all writing), it has also, in its move to Brennan's essay, introduced a type of writing that more closely resembles the kind of "essay" you may be accustomed to writing in your courses: It is the type of essay that presents a point of view or an argument and marshals evidence in support of it.

As we hope the example of Brennan's work suggests, the kind of writing about difficulty called forth in the Difficulty Paper can serve as valuable "prewriting" work for this more traditional academic essay. But how is the writer to undertake this transition? The major difference between the "difficulty paper" and the "academic essay" may lie in the extent to which the writer is prepared to share his or her difficulties; that is, whether those difficulties are to be understood as predominantly the property of the self (and hence personal and idiosyncratic) or others (hence public and communal). When a writer acquires the confidence to claim (or activates a perspective that makes the announcing of such a claim seem important) that what he or she is experiencing as a reader is also in all likelihood being experienced by other readers, that writer can then form a hypothesis whose merit is demonstrable through citation, through the presentation of textual evidence.

Let us classify a few of the differences in this way:

The Difficulty Paper	The Academic Essay
Presents a reader engaged in the process of reading	Presents a reader who has completed a "reading"
Describes the difficulties encountered by a single reader in the reading process	Defines the challenges encountered by the "general" reader
Cites from the text, in order to make its examination of difficulty more specific	Cites from the text to provide evidence of the claims made above
Places a text within the "context" of a single reader's interpretive experience	Places a text within the "context"of a general practice of reading; may also situate the text in a larger context (that of gender, ethnicity, history, theoretical problem, textual and/or literary study) in order to make its difficulties part of a larger analysis of or argument about these categories

Understanding the "Reading and Writing" Transaction

As we mentioned at the beginning of the chapter, our plan was to reverse the direction of the previous chapters by moving from writing to reading, rather than from reading to writing. We asked you to reflect on a type of writing you have in all likelihood generated and then reflect on how that experience shaped your reading of text that belongs to the same general category, the category of the explicitly personal. This reversal of motion enables us to capture more precisely than before the interdependence of reading and writing, the nature of their *transaction.* What does that mean? It means that reading a text is essentially a form of rewriting that text that highlights certain features and not others. And writing a text (personal narrative, analytical essay, historical account) is essentially a form of reading (the self, a text, an experience) that highlights some features rather than others.

But in each case, which features are to be highlighted? In college courses, what you choose to highlight when reading and rewriting, when writing and rereading, may be determined by the work your teacher wants you to undertake. But you may also have purposes of your own. What might they be? And what kind of textual features will they lead you to highlight? How can you attend to the assigned task, and your inclinations, in ways that one does not obstruct the other?

Taking Stock

Because we have done a different kind of work in these pages, we will conclude with different questions that focus on your experience with Montaigne. But we will also ask you to think about what you have learned so far in other chapters.

- "You have here an essay of my natural parts not of those acquired." What does this mean, and what does it allow Montaigne to say about reading and writing books?
- "I do not pretend to discover things but to lay open myself." What preunderstandings about the subjects he reads, and what assumptions about reading and writing history does Montaigne "lay open"?
- Connelly raised the issue of the difficulty of intertextuality in her comments about quotations and references. How does Montaigne use and mark borrowings from other texts? Why? What lesson can you glean from this?
- Montaigne alludes to the difficulty of remembering all that he reads. What strategies does he devise to support his "want of memory"? What system of notation? What do his comments about memory suggest about the workings of memory in the reading process?
- "Only to please myself by an honest diversion." Since he likes to read for diversion, Montaigne often gives up on the difficulties he encounters. He

has that luxury. What if he were a classmate of yours and he had to reflect on the reasons for and the interpretive potential of his difficulties?

- Check what he says about Guicciardini, Ariosto, and Cicero. What does he see in how they write, and why? What does he not see, and why? How could you teach Montaigne to "lay open" the goods of these texts?
- What is the difference between reading for pleasure and reading for learning? What makes reading for learning pleasurable? What can make pleasurable reading a learning experience?

Retrospective

This chapter builds on the work of the previous chapters by examining the production of prose in a nonfictional genre—the personal essay. This chapter also reverses the direction of others chapters in that it asks you to reflect on the writing you tend to do, on what you learned about reading *and* writing from those experiences, and then apply that pre-understanding to your reading of an essay by Montaigne, the creator of the *essai* as an instrument of self-examination. The purpose of this move is to emphasize the idea that, as a *practitioner* of the personal essay, you know something about, and can draw upon your understanding of, this genre, even as you read an instantiation of it by Montaigne. This chapter also picks up on issues discussed in previous chapters: What kind of "truth value" do stories have and how do reading and writing relate to each other? And it asks you to reflect on the differences between the personal essay and the type of writing you are commonly called upon to produce in the college classroom—the academic essay.

7

A Provisional Conclusion

[T]eaching readers to read "dialogically"—viewing the text as an intentionally crafted product of an author, attempting to create a particular effect on a reader. This dialogic reading requires readers to understand the effects a text has on them, what literary conventions define such effects, how the text comes to mean in terms of their personal identities, and how the text reflects the values, norms, and expectations of particular cultures.

—Susan Hynds, *"Questions of Difficulty in Literary Reading"*

American culture does not take well to the idea of difficulty. Our penchant is for one-step, one-stop solutions to problems, and we expect and demand in all areas of life, including reading, an ease of achievement that is antithetical to thought itself...The quest for solutions is synonymous with a reductiveness that leaves aside the problematic movement of thought. Students often tackle "education" as if it were a puzzle to be considered solved when every piece is in place. But an education—or reading—worthy of its name will recognize that when the puzzle is finally put together into a perfect whole, there is always one piece left over which forces us to rethink the edifice we have erected.

—Helen Reguiero Elam, *"The Difficulty of Reading"*

In this chapter, we will add one last *new* difficulty to this list, one seldom framed for undergraduates as worth exploring, although it is one that in the last three decades has produced some of the most consequential reflections on reading literary texts. It is the difficulty generated by a text that has already in a sense been predigested *for* readers, a text that comes to readers with a package of pre-understandings attached to the author's name. In the 1940s, I.A.Richards preceded the question of an author's influence in a famous study of undergraduates' responses to highly reputed literary texts, whose names had been deleted. It might interest you to know that some venerated authors did not receive high scores!

Reading a "Great" Author

> The difficulty with the difficulty in Shakespeare is the man himself.
>
> —Casey Lyons

Our goal so far has been to persuade you to trust the difficulties you experience as a reader, to reflect on their nature, and to turn them into strategies of interpretation. In this chapter, we will consider the name "William Shakespeare" as a difficulty. What obstacles arise when an author's reputation overrides a reader's creativity and keeps in check his or her interpretive strategies?

How can readers trust the difficulties they experience with a Shakespearean text and look at them as moments of insight into what the text is asking them to do, rather than signs of imaginative inadequacy, lack of knowledge, insufficient preparation? Focusing on Shakespeare will also allow us to reflect on some of the difficulties that punctuate the reading of drama, the genre with which Shakespeare is mostly identified. What happens when readers read drama (plays) with expectations of story, character, and language conventions suited to poetry or narrative, to fiction or nonfiction? On the other hand, how can their understanding of these conventions be put to fruitful use?

Let us begin, as usual, with a few exploratory questions. As you engage them, consider what they are supposed to lead you to assess. Remember that our purpose in asking questions throughout has not been to lead you to pre-established conclusions. Rather, we have asked and continue to ask questions to activate as many pre-understandings, sediments of knowledge, traces of assumptions as possible since they affect, mostly in deceptive ways, our understandings. As Hans-Georg Gadamer says, "The operation of the understanding requires that the unconscious elements involved in the original act of knowledge be brought to consciousness" (45).

How does a story told by Shakespeare differ from a story told by a writer who, although famous, might not be familiar to you, or by somebody from your circle of friends, or somebody you do not know at all?

While some of the authors whose books we mentioned may be new to you, that is probably not the case with William Shakespeare. Even if you never read any of his plays, so closely is Shakespeare's name associated with literary study, especially the study of English literature, that it is difficult to conceive of one without the other.

We ask you to begin your work in this chapter by recalling (re-collecting) the knowledge of Shakespeare you already possess, by virtue of having read his plays in school or seen them in performance, or of living in a culture where the name of Shakespeare is highly revered.

- Who is William Shakespeare?
- When and where did he live?
- Have you ever seen a picture or a statue of him? How is he represented?
- Have you read, or seen, or heard of any of his plays?
- How would you characterize your response to them?
- If you used the word "great" in your responses so far, explain the term. Assess if this determination of his "greatness" is something you thought on your own, something you heard, or something that was inculcated in you by others, such as teachers.
- Why do you think Shakespeare's works are taught in school? If you were not required to read his plays in school, would you choose to read them on your own? Why or why not?
- Make a list of authors you consider great. How did you decide? Which categories emerge from your list?

The critic Harold Bloom speaks of Shakespeare as the "center" of the Western **canon**. In his book *The Western Canon,* Bloom makes the claims listed below. As you read them, consider the following questions: Have you heard similar claims before? Are they meaningful to you? Do you understand them? For each of the questions, explain why or why not.

- "No other writer has ever had Shakespeare's resources of language, which are so florabundant in *Love's Labour's Lost* that we feel many of the limits of language have been reached, once and for all" (47).
- "Shakespeare's greatest originality is in representation of character...."(47).
- "Coming to Shakespeare after writing about Romantic and modern poets and after meditating on the issues of influence and originality, I experience the shock of difference...the shock of a verbal art larger and more definitive than any other, so persuasive that it seems to be not art at all but something that was always there" (47).
- "Shakespeare is the Canon. He sets the standard and the limits of literature" (48).
- "The Shakespearean exuberance or gusto is part of what breaks through linguistic or cultural barriers. You cannot confine Shakespeare to the English Renaissance...."(52).
- "Shakespeare has the largeness of nature itself...."(52).
- "Rhetorically, Shakespeare has no equal; no more awesome panoply of metaphor exists" (60).

Respond to each of the above statements. Do they sound familiar? What does it mean to speak of a writer as revealing the "limits of language," as being "original" in his representation of character, of utilizing language in ways that seem not "artful" but natural, "always there"? Does it make sense to you to say that a writer contains "the largeness of nature itself"?

If these ideas make sense to you, perhaps even resonate with your own experience, how might they affect how you read Shakespeare's plays, and how you work through their difficulties? What kinds of expectations do such statements create? In what ways do your expectations of Shakespeare's texts affect your reading of them? Try to apply these statements to any of the authors on the list of "greats" you have constructed.

Write a class memo to Bloom. Ask questions that will make him explain, and reflect on, his position on Shakespeare and the ensuing valuations of him.

Becoming Aware of Shakespeare's Aura

> Reflection on a given pre-understanding brings before me something that otherwise happens *behind my back.*
>
> —Hans-Georg Gadamer

In a recent class on literary criticism at Lafayette College, students were asked to revise Difficulty Papers on Shakespeare's *Othello* written during the first week of the semester. In their first encounter with difficulty, students found the concept of difficulty itself unsettling, fuzzy. As good English majors and students in their junior and senior years, they had acquired considerable facility in their reading of challenging materials. They tended to ignore what did not make sense, focusing on what was clear and presenting their knowledge in the form of carefully crafted and supported arguments. Their purpose as writers was to demonstrate interpretive mastery; quite often, they succeeded. Therefore, being asked to reflect on difficulty struck them as a peculiar, maybe even demeaning, exercise. They were, eventually, able to embrace the project's challenges and see its merits. And yet, when later on in the term they were asked to return to the first piece of writing and to revise it in light of acquired understanding, their exploration of difficulty once again proved difficult, although in different ways than before.

In case you have not read *Othello*, a brief plot summary might be helpful. And please keep in mind that a summary of a plot is itself an interpretation, a particular kind of thread tracing. In this play, the title character is a highly successful general who has done great service for the city of Venice, even though he is not a citizen of the city itself. He is an outsider, a Moor (a word signifying many things at once—an African, a person of mixed Arab-Berber descent, a Muslim, someone who is "black"). As we learn from Othello himself in Act I, as a distinguished general of a mercenary army, he had been a frequent guest at the home of Brabantio, one of the city's nobles, where he would share stories of his wondrous adventures. Brabantio's daughter, Desdemona, overheard these stories; and gradually she and Othello fell in love and secretly married—an event that shocked Brabantio and other city nobles (for not only is Othello an outsider and a Moor, he is also considerably older than Desdemona). After an informal trial of sorts, during which Othello is asked by Brabantio and the Venetian Duke to prove that he has not "charmed" Desdemona (Desdemona speaks in his defense) and is, of course, successful, Othello is asked to depart immediately for Cyprus to defend that island against the Turks. Desdemona asks to accompany him, and her safety is placed in the hands of Othello's long-standing lieutenant, Iago. Once on Cyprus, Iago, whose jealousy of Othello and Desdemona and also of Cassio (a soldier whom Othello has promoted over Iago) is limitless and irrational (the poet Coleridge, to whom you have already been introduced, described Iago's actions as deriving from a "motiveless malignity"), plots to destroy all three. Gradually and with considerable deliberation, he is able to persuade Othello that Desdemona has been unfaithful to him with Cassio, which is, of course, a lie. In Act V, Othello kills Desdemona and then, learning of his terrible error from Iago's own wife, kills himself. Iago remains alive at the end of the play—alive but silent.

With that summary in mind, read the following comments:

> The first difficulty I had in reading the passage, beginning on line 127, was Othello's immediate reference to Brabantio's contradictory emotions towards him, as compared to his past reaction several lines before...I do not understand why Brabantio would so quickly alter his opinion of a man he so admired just because his daughter became involved with him, the local hero. (Emily Ginsberg)

> Iago is utterly deceptive and uses all his wit and skill to accomplish his own self-serving agenda, while Othello appears blissfully calm in the face of adversity. While Othello's tranquility may not seem unnatural at first, once we examine the character of Iago, it becomes clear that Othello should recognize the conspiracies against him. (Matt Parrott)

Emily Ginsberg finds it peculiar that a father would change his opinion of a man he admired "just because" that man became "involved" with his daughter (that Othello and Desdemona differ greatly in terms of culture, race, age, background, and life experience does not seem to be relevant to her). Matt Parrott thinks that Othello should have recognized Iago's intrigue (even though Othello and Iago share a strong bond as military compatriots). What is the nature of the difficulties these students identify? How would you describe them in relationship to those we have seen elsewhere in this book?

While it happens in "life" that fathers are suspicious of the men their daughters love and that men trust their male friends more than their wives, these students seem surprised by these occurrences. Here the *ordinary* is transformed into something *extraordinary*. Why?

Consider whose text these students are reading. Which frameworks of prior understanding do they bring to it? Which codes of behavior? What kind of understanding do they achieve by moving to the realm of the "extraordinary"? What does the "extraordinary" free them from saying?

In a subsequent piece of writing, students in this class were asked to reflect on the figure of Shakespeare himself, on his name, and the associations that it carries. They were asked to reflect on Shakespeare's **aura,** on the high esteem with which they regarded him.

I think perhaps this awkwardness in approaching Shakespeare, in attempting to analyze and therefore break down his works, stems from intimidation about his reputation. He is revered, so why untangle something considered to be so well-thought out already? (Emily Ginsberg)

Shakespeare has always been presented to me as the greatest author of the greatest plays ever written in the English language. But like many other "great authors," I find myself not reading [him] casually. I'm always aware, at least in the periphery, that it's a "great" author I'm reading, and not Joe Schmo. As such, I don't think I'm really able to get into the text...I think that the difficulty lies in the difference between the acclaim that the work receives and how much I actually enjoy the work. (Tim Fargus)

We began reading Shakespeare in 10th grade and continued to read him throughout high school, more so than other authors. With this intense high school emphasis...I have been raised to believe Shakespeare is in a sense a God of Writing...When I read Shakespeare, I search for everything and anything in his work that would explain the title...I do not approach the text as a reader wanting a reading experience; instead, I am a reader trying to conquer a task: the task of finding in the text [what will allow me] to understand why he is so great. (Heather Bastian)

The difficulty with the difficulty in Shakespeare is the man himself... Going into any Shakespeare reading, a reader almost feels forced to like his writing, or at least find parts that he/she likes. (Casey Lyons)

Perhaps as a reader [of Shakespeare] I am more inclined to internalize difficulties...rather than find them in the text, because of the respect and aura of his plays. (Brendan Cotter)

It is difficult to talk about the difficulty in reading Shakespeare because we have been conditioned to see him as great and irreproachable. His text we see as beyond criticism...If I don't understand...this reflects badly upon me. (Brandt Siegel)

My understanding (learned) of the name "Shakespeare" is "great writer," often "greatest writer of all time." My experience with Shakespeare, however, is different. I expect enlightening and grand statements about humanity, but I find simplistic characters that are often allegorical and unreal to me. I'm having difficulty determining what's so great about Shakespeare, and perhaps that is because my expectations are too high. (Erin Wyble)

Circle and connect the words of praise that appear in all these texts.

- What themes can you glean from these stories of reading?
- What patterns emerge?
- Do they echo your ideas about Shakespeare?

Hearing Cultural Noise

In the preceding chapters, we have encouraged you to tap into what you already know, so that you can approach and make sense of texts that may otherwise seem unfamiliar or difficult. Here, as you approach the difficulties of a text by Shakespeare, we are asking that you consider whether and why, in the case of an author like Shakespeare, it might be wise to check what you already know about him at the door.

Obviously, we are encouraging you to make what is called an *iconoclastic* move. (Check the meaning of the word, and consider how the meaning of "icon" has changed by the time it appears in computer language.) Although this move might seem anathema to some, consistent with our approach throughout, we are trying to alert you to the fact that sometimes the knowledge, the information that circulates *outside* a text like *Othello* can impinge upon a reading of it in ways we might want to control. That is, while it is always the case, as we mentioned in the introduction, that a reader brings to texts a repertoire of expectations, experiences, and knowledge (whether implicit or explicit) which she can use to negotiate a meaning (no reading is ever "pure" or "original"), that repertoire may produce so much noise that alternative readings are inhibited. Such seems to be the case with this expectation of greatness. But we can make a similar case with any negative reputation that precedes a text, a person, an event.

For the moment, please read the following excerpt, thinking about what the writer, Emily Ginsberg, is doing. Notice where she begins.

- How does she position herself in relation to the play?
- What knowledge does she "re-collect" to aid her entry into this text?
- Is her starting point *Othello* or something else?
- What is the function of the move she is making? What does that move enable her to do?

As a first time reader of *Othello,* but seasoned reader of Shakespeare, I had minor difficulties following the plot of the first Act. However, there are certain aspects within the play that were soon brought to my attention as I continued exploring the story line.

To begin, the notion of Brabantio being "robbed" of his sole daughter leads to the idea that Desdemona, representative of a woman in the 17th century, is looked upon unjustly as a piece of property to be owned by men (never mind their personal relationship to her).

Brabantio, as her father, seems to want custody of her forever, like she is a prized possession of great worth. [After] her marriage to Othello [is confirmed], their lust for each other becomes evident; and therefore Desdemona is regarded as an object for pleasure as well. We, as readers, know little of her mind, nor her ability to place power behind her words. She is not allowed that luxury often (the privilege of speaking her mind), save for the moment she argues against her father's wishes to be reconsidered in his eyes as Othello's wife, a woman of new title. This seems proof of the manner in which women were treated during that era, as Shakespeare has conveyed to us in his writing. The question thus arises. Will this continue to play out as a twisted sort of love story, as men of power continually volley for her affections? Or, will Desdemona overcome the cookie-cutter image in which she has been portrayed and develop into a stronger and highly revered character as the drama continues.

While Emily Ginsberg is producing a reading with important implications, a reading that interprets Desdemona as "property," it is also a reading that configures the play as an example of a historical phenomenon. (You may find our discussion of history in Chapter 3 helpful.) What is the prior historical knowledge Ginsberg brings to this task? What understanding does that make possible? What does it prevent her from considering? Can you imagine another point of beginning?

In the earlier excerpts, students transformed ordinary experiences into extraordinary ones. Is Ginsberg using a different interpretive strategy? What does that strategy enable her to do? If Desdemona is considered as "representative" of a seventeenth-century woman, what kind of analysis of her character might be precluded by Ginsberg's moves?

Understanding Shakespeare's Characters

> Shakespeare's greatest originality is in representation of character.
>
> —Harold Bloom

> Character is a central concept in traditional approaches to narrative, especially novels, plays and film. That is why the meaning and the value of the term are often merely assumed or asserted.
>
> —Rob Pope

Bloom is talking specifically about Shakespeare, Pope about "common" understandings of "character." But where does what they say come from? For we who live after Shakespeare grew to be so great, are "common," that is, "shared," understandings of character independent of what established, authoritative readers of Shakespeare have put in circulation?

We are not suggesting that you have to toss away, or be suspicious of any of the notions about Shakespeare you have absorbed just by going to school, or living the life you have lived. But we want to make sure that you become conscious of how those notions might trigger certain automatic readings of the play, and that you do not find yourself "merely assum[ing] or assert[ing] them." In other words, we want you to be conscious of the consequences of such assumptions and assertions for *your* interpretations.

> Character: [ME carecter < Lat. character < Gk. kharacter < kharassein, to inscribe.]
>
> Character derives from a Greek word meaning "to engrave, to inscribe" and currently has three main meanings:
>
> 1. the distinctive nature, disposition and traits of a real person (e.g., "My children have/are quite different characters");
> 2. the particular role played by a fictional figure in a novel, film or play (e.g., "Hamlet is a character in Shakespeare's play of that name");
> 3. a letter of the alphabet or other graphic device (e.g., "The printer picked up each character and put it in its box").
>
> —Rob Pope

After you think through what these quotations enable us to think about character, go back to the previous section, and re-read what Ginsberg says about Desdemona: "We, as readers, know little of her mind, nor her ability to place power behind her words. She is not allowed that luxury often (the privilege of speaking her mind), save for the moment she argues against her father's wishes to be reconsidered in his eyes as Othello's wife, a woman of new title."

Ginsberg is pointing to two important conventions of plays: We know characters, we make assumptions and conclusions about characters, on the basis of their words and their actions. Characters reveal their inner selves in dialogue with others. But their strength, their "character" can only be measured through action—the acts they perform, the acts by which they affect the outcome of the storyline.

Make a list of the narrative resources available to Steedman and Danticat, and of the linguistic resources Montaigne could rely on to build an argument, take a position, change a perspective. Now think about a play, any play, you have read. Are these resources transferable to drama? How can a playwright use these resources within the confines of the genre? What changes must be made, and why? For a play to be a play, what conventions must be relied upon, even if only to be transgressed? And finally, what can you conclude about the conventions and their power both to enable and to interdict?

Considering the Author Function

In the excerpts presented above, we see that expectations readers bring to a text may very well interfere with their reading of it by setting up certain kinds of goals to be met that are a measure of the text's "worth." The text is then "rewritten," either to conform to those expectations ("Isn't this/am I not great") or to undermine them ("This isn't/I am not so great").

In Ginsberg's text, we see a character being read as an example of a historical type. Desdemona is read as an example of the fact that women, at that particular historical time, were not allowed much freedom in word and action, rather than as a possible example of a playwright's inadequate knowledge of women's psychology, motivations, strengths, desires. Which/whose kind of knowledge is being activated here? What does this knowledge make the reader see (and ignore) in the text she is reading?

The ways of reading that these students exemplify is one given considerable attention by Michel Foucault, a historian and theorist. He refers to it as the **author function,** and he has the following to say in the essay, "What Is An Author?" You might find it comforting to know that we all struggled with this essay and with all of Michel Foucault's work. But he gave us a different compass. We want you to have this experience much earlier than we did.

> ...we can briefly consider the problems that arise in the use of an author's name. What is the name of an author? How does it function? Far from offering a solution, I will attempt to indicate some of the difficulties related to these questions.
>
> ...an author's name is not simply an element of speech (as a subject, a complement, or an element that could be replaced by a pronoun or other parts of speech). Its presence is functional in that it serves as a means of classification. A name can group together a number of texts and thus differentiate them from others. A name also establishes different forms of relationships among texts....Finally, the author's name characterizes a particular manner of existence of discourse. Discourse that possesses an author's name is not to be immediately consumed and forgotten: neither is it accorded the momentary attention given to ordinary, fleeting words. Rather, its status and its manner of reception are regulated by the culture in which it circulates.
>
> We can conclude that, unlike a proper name, which moves from the interior of a discourse to the real person outside who produced it, the name of the author remains at the contours of texts—separating one from the other, defining the form, and characterizing their mode of existence. It points to the existence of certain groups of discourse and refers to the status of this discourse within a society and culture. The author's name is not a function of a man's civil status, nor is it fictional; it is situated in the breach, among the discontinuities, which gives rise to new groups of discourse and their singular mode of existence.... In this sense, the function of an author is to characterize the existence, circulation, and operation of certain discourses within a society. (*Norton Anthology,* 1626–28).

What Foucault helps us to understand—as did our student writers—is that an author's name is a construct. Unlike the name of Edwidge Danticat, for example (but that will soon change), the name of "Shakespeare" is a constellation of prior and potential understandings, an accretion of characteristics and features—stylistic, discursive, historical. In *Romeo and Juliet,* the question is posed—"What's in a name?" The example of William Shakespeare would suggest, "virtually everything."

Confronting Shakespeare's Name

We want to look at two Difficulty Papers by Heather Bastian and Brendan Cotter that confront the problem of Shakespeare's name in various ways. Since both excerpts respond to the same moment in the play, we present it below. It is an early scene, where Othello explains to Desdemona's father and the Duke of Venice how he came to win the hand of Desdemona without recourse, as they fear, to witchcraft or a magical potion. As you read, note your moments of difficulty. Are you able to engage this passage as easily as others in this book? That is, do any of your preconceptions about Shakespeare or his "art" affect your attempts to negotiate the text?

> Her father loved me, oft invited me,
> Still questioned me the story of my life
> From year to year—the battles, sieges, fortunes
> That I have passed.
> I ran it through, even from my boyish days
> To the very moment that he bade me tell it;
> Wherein I spake of most disastrous chances,
> Of moving accidents by flood and field,
> Of hair-breadth scapes i'th'imminent deadly breach,
> Of being taken by the insolent foe
> And sold to slavery; of my redemption thence,
> And with it all my travels' history:
> Wherein of antres vast and deserts idle,
> Rough quarries, rocks, and hills whose heads touch
> heaven,
> It was my hint to speak—such was the process:
> And of the cannibals that each other eat,
> The Anthropophagi, and men whose heads
> Do grow beneath their shoulders. This to hear
> Would Desdemona seriously incline;
> But still the house affairs would draw her thence,
> Which ever as she could with haste dispatch
> She'd come again, and with a greedy ear

Devour up my discourse; which I observing
Took once a pliant hour and found good means
To draw from her a prayer of earnest heart
That I would all my pilgrimage dilate
Whereof by parcels she had something heard,
But not intentively. I did consent,
And often did beguile her of her tears
When I did speak of some distressful stroke
That my youth suffered. My story being done,
She gave me for my pains a world of sighs:
She swore, in faith, 'twas strange, 'twas passing strange,
'Twas pitiful, 'twas pitiful;
She wished she had not heard it, yet she wished
That heaven hath made her such a man. She thanked me,
And bade me, if I had a friend that loved her,
I should but teach him how to tell my story,
And that would woo her. Upon this hint I spake:
She loved me for the dangers I had passed,
And I loved her that she did pity them.
This only is the witchcraft I have used.
Here comes the lady: let her witness it. (I,iii, 127–169)

"chances": events
"by flood and field": on sea and on land
"antres": caves
"Anthropophagi": man-eaters, cannibals
"pliant": favorable
"intentively": altogether
"passing": exceedingly
"learn me": teach me

One of the most common and plausible difficulties readers experience with Shakespearean texts is the Elizabethan language. We do not deny its disorienting power. Therefore, we have "glossed" some of the words that by now are no longer or differently used. We would like however for you to trace, in whatever form or shape, the transformation of your thinking as you move from the specific point in Shakespeare's text, as we have abstracted it into our text, to the glossary, and back to that point. Try to capture and reflect on the expansion of meanings produced by the moves you make as you do this seemingly simple exercise.

In working through this passage, were you able to draw on any prior understanding of literary conventions? What about your understanding of the story/plot distinction? This is a narrative moment in the play, the kind of moment that seems antithetical to the spirit of drama, which is that of showing, rather than relating. We have here another case of hybridity and we want you to explore how the function and the effects of narrative change when it is based on series of fragmented, related, interpolated, or unrelated actions. Who does the filling and connecting of the gaps between actions and thoughts?

Heather Bastian

Let us now consider how a student writer, Heather Bastian, responded to this passage. As you read her Difficulty Paper, use the strategies you have employed elsewhere: for example, circling words dense with assumptions. Pay attention to the interpretive moves she makes. How does she engage with the "author problem"?

Note: I tried to focus on why I had the difficulty, my reaction to the difficulty, and the questions the difficulty caused me to pose. I am not sure if I have this down yet, but I wanted to let you know what I was trying to get across in an effort to see if I actually achieved this goal. Thank you.

Within Othello's story of wooing Desdemona, clear contradictions between Othello's actions and words are apparent to me, and these contradictions caused difficulty when I was reading this section. First, before Othello begins his tale of wooing, one of the first things he states is, "Rude am I in speech/And little blessed with soft phrase of peace..." Since Othello is saying that he is rude in speech, I would think that he would not try to persuade the senators through language, yet he does. It seems odd to me that someone who truly believes that he/she does not use language well would use language to persuade others. It appears as though Shakespeare is making Othello present himself as something he is not (an inarticulate man), but why would he do this? Furthermore, why would Shakespeare have Othello say this, then contradict himself by speaking in eloquent and articulate language? Since Othello says that he cannot speak well, yet does, this indicates to me as a reader that it is important that he first degrades himself. At this point, I encountered this difficulty of trying to figure out why Shakespeare would have Othello say he acts in one manner then have Othello actually act in the opposite manner; and more so, why is Shakespeare placing such an emphasis upon language. Why is language so important in this passage?

In order to resolve this problem, I read on in an effort to discern why Shakespeare would do this; however, my initial difficulty becomes more complicated when Othello begins this tale of wooing. He begins his tale by stating, "Her father loved me, oft invited me, still questioning me the story of my life." Why would someone who is rude in speech be asked to share the story of his life? Since Othello has already established himself as rude in speech, I did not expect him to say that others want to hear him speak his stories. Once again, it appears as if Othello is not rude in speech, even though he says he is. This makes me further question Shakespeare's choice to have Othello say one thing, yet portray him in another light. The importance of his initial statement takes on more weight (due to the further demonstration of his proficiency in language), yet I still do not understand why he would place so much emphasis upon language.

Still confused, I read further, hoping that at some point I could resolve this difficulty; but again, as his tale continues, the language issue gains even more importance. Othello not only has shown that he is not rude in speech by using language well and by saying that others wished to hear his story, but also Desdemona was attracted to him because of his speech. Othello states, "[His stories] to hear would Desdemona seriously inclined...She'd come again, and with a greedy ear devour my discourse." Once again, if someone was rude in speech, I do not believe that a member of the opposite sex would come to him or her and "devour" the discourse. At this point, Shakespeare seems to have demolished Othello's first words that he is rude in speech by proving that Othello won the hearts of man, also Desdemona, through his stories. Since most of this story and even his words themselves are focused on his use of language, this further indicates to me that language usage is profoundly important, yet I am still in the dark as to why it is important.

In an effort to resolve this difficulty, I could further read *Othello* in detail and reread the previous sections; however, I am unsure if they would help me fully resolve this difficulty. In the previous paper, I wrote about how Othello is also presented as a beast-like man, but then proves himself to be quite civilized; therefore, the initial negative impression of Othello, then the tearing down of the impression, seems to be prevalent in this play. How am I to resolve these difficulties? My initial response would be to ask myself what did Shakespeare intend to imply by creating these contradictions, but I see this as a digression from my difficulty. It is my difficulty so why should I look to an author as having some divine reason for presenting Othello in this manner? Am I not in control of my difficulty and its resolution? I acknowledged these contradictions, and I can choose to ignore them or just say well, Shakespeare did it for a reason, what was *his* reason? Instead, I am inclined to focus on why I believe this is in the text. By focusing on my reasons, I force myself to think as a writer. If I were to have written this text, why would I present these contradictions? Why would language be an important aspect for a writer to focus on? To me, this would lead to a successful resolution because I place myself in the writer's position, and I could resolve my difficulty through my own thoughts (which I can confirm), instead of focusing on what I believe another person wanted me to think (which can never be confirmed).

Still, my idea of how to resolve my difficulties makes me think outside of Shakespeare the author, which I acknowledge is hard because of yet another difficulty I face when reading Shakespeare: my previous expectations and ideas about Shakespeare the author. Quite possibly the first author I ever heard of was Shakespeare; and growing up, all I ever heard was how great Shakespeare is as an author, and his works were so influential and important. Therefore, when I read Shakespeare, I force myself to think that he must be trying to represent something that is outside my understanding. More so, I believe that since he is supposed to be a great author, all of his works contain great meanings that I usually just do not "get." The "repertoire" I bring to Shakespeare forces me to look beyond the text and look for something brilliant that Shakespeare intended. Still, if I think about it, I should not be afraid of Shakespeare because of the "repertoire" that has been created for him. He is still an author, still a human, and still open to as many faults as other great writers. Whether I am reading Shakespeare or a Lafayette College student's work, I will always encounter difficulties. And much like when I read a student's work I do not look for what [he or she] meant to intend, I should not look for what Shakespeare meant to intend. I need to look to the words and my own thought processes to create the "meaning." Language then becomes the real difficulty, not the author's intentions, and Shakespeare is not more "difficult" to read than other words by great authors.

Brendan Cotter

Before we proceed to Taking Stock, we provide one last Difficulty Paper on Shakespeare. As you read it, bring into play, recall and rearticulate, the range of difficulties you have examined in this chapter. Be especially attentive to the moves that produce Cotter's text. At which moments do ideas of "reputation," "fame," and "author's name" interfere with his ability—and desire—to construct the text as a "story" about his experience as a reader? How is he able to negotiate these ideas, move beyond them, silence their "noise"? Which of these moves could you see yourself employing in reading "great" texts by "illustrious" authors?

I ran into two main interpretive difficulties in Shakespeare's *Othello* that caused me to stop and wonder why the play was not holding together. As the play progressed, I too was putting together the story as I read it. However, there were points when I felt I could not make out a coherent story. At these stopping points, I didn't feel I had been given enough information to explain what I saw happening. I encountered my first difficulty in Act I, when I read through the Senate's reaction to Othello. After initially being exposed to a negative cultural response to Othello's race, I stopped when the Senate reacted differently to him. They laud him as a military hero, and clearly are not as critical as Brabantio (himself a member of the Senate). Also, there seems to be a mixed reaction within Brabantio himself that comes out when Othello tells the story of his courtship with Desdemona. My second difficulty occurred when reading through Othello's ignorance of Iago's deception in Acts III and IV. Throughout the play I had to fight my knowledge of Iago with everyone else's ignorance of that knowledge. Yet because Othello had been introduced to me as a careful reader of character, I simply could not accept his obvious blindness later on. How would I resolve these difficulties? In answering this question a critical theory of literature emerges.

The initial scenes with Iago, Roderigo, and Brabantio laid the groundwork for a racist response to Othello. In their language, I could easily pick out motivations for their hatred. Roderigo labels him "the thick lips" while Iago refers to him as "an old black ram" and "a Barbary horse" (7). When they tell Brabantio of Desdemona's love for him, he too responds racially, accusing Othello of black magic in taking Desdemona's heart. He claims that the Moor had used magic and deceit to lure his daughter away from him "though has enchanted her," he says, and wonders why Desdemona would "fall in love with what she feared to look on" (29)....

Shakespeare's plot seems to be carelessly thrown together, containing stories that do not agree with previous information. As a reader I go into a Shakespeare play with a great deal of respect for what is written, so when I am forced to stop at certain contradictory points of the play my reading is disrupted.

The second difficulty occurred as I read through the later acts and watched Othello be deceived by Iago. Again I had to stop because an initial assumption about the play and its characters was turned on its head.... My reading was stopped by Othello's obvious ignorance and quick temper. I couldn't resolve this with what I had already established as a reader of earlier actions in the play. He allows Iago's shallow story, based merely on a handkerchief, to lead him to kill what he loved most. Othello, the perfect reader in Act I, suddenly becomes the worst reader in the play. Why? The story itself seems to provide no explanation and finishes with a disgraced Othello and murdered Desdemona....

Taking Stock

When I first came into this class I discovered that the main portion of writing assignments was to focus on our personal difficulties with individual poems. The first couple of assignments were comprehensible because we would describe our problem and the professor would help us solve it. Then we were asked to locate difficulties as before, but we were also asked to solve them. I was extremely confused as to how we could answer our own questions.... [That's when Kim consults the dictionary and discovers that a difficulty is an obstacle.] This made me realize that the difficulties I have in understanding poetry can be overcome with some extra work. Through this extra work I personally have discovered certain strategies that help me overcome my obstacles. (Kim Woomer)

- We used this excerpt by Kim Woomer in the Introduction. Do you remember the effect it had on you? Which of her statements did you find yourself in agreement with, and why? Which of her statements surprised you or aroused your suspicion? Did you find this early definition and assessment of difficulty useful? How do you interpret our move to include Woomer's text at that point?
- Look back at this book. Highlight places in it that marked moments of insight. Block places that caused confusion, resistance, perplexity, tedium. Look back at the work you produced in this course. Mark places in your writing that represent moments of insight as well as confusion, resistance, perplexity, tedium.
- Write an essay in which—weaving quotations from these two sources and from others, if you want—you give an account of how you read and worked through this book, and with which consequences. The purpose of this essay is to give your teacher well-thought demonstrations of what you have learned. Do not tell what your writing cannot show.

OR:

- Write a dramatic dialogue, or a conversation about reading, constructing characters, naming them, and making them say things that indicate recognizable positions on reading.

OR:

- Set up a Double-Entry Notebook. In one column, identify and comment on the terms and concepts we introduced in the previous chapter that made you think the most. In the next column, identify and comment on the terms and concepts that confused you the most. Is there any correlation between the two sets of terms?

  As we said earlier, these are terms and concepts by some of the most difficult theorists of reading we ourselves had to engage as scholars. Try to articulate those difficulties as fully and creatively as you can.

OR:

- Using the system of notation you have developed to mark the texts you have examined so far, think of how you might want to describe your reading process:

  1. Consider the patterns of reading your notations make visible. What kind of moves do you tend to make as you read a text?

2. Look at your notes, your writing, your marginalia: Make a list of the literary terms you took notice of, or relied on as you worked throughout the term.
3. Free-write on the following terms: "genius," "imagination," "inspiration," and "creativity."
4. Go to a dictionary. Check the terms. Consider how many of the dictionary meanings you used—that is, consider how much you relied on the term's **polysemy.** Did the term's polysemy confuse you? Why or why not?
5. Focus on moments when you came to understand genius, imagination, inspiration, and creativity *differently*.
6. Then, keeping all of the above in mind, write an autobiographical narrative in which you define and explain the relations between reading, *understanding*, and *difficulty* on the basis of the work you have done in this course.

And finally, for revisions of this book, please think carefully about the following question: As we have addressed you so far, what did we not take into account that we might have or should have?

We promise to include the most fruitful suggestions in future editions of this book.

Retrospective

In place of our usual retrospective, which we have used to summarize and to place in final perspective the emphases of a single chapter, we ask you to offer a retrospective of the entire book, in the form of two lists. In the first list, you should summarize the major difficulties examined throughout this book and the chapters where such a discussion occurs (please note that certain difficulties, like those of "mismatch," are touched upon in almost every chapter). In the second list, you should summarize the strategies you developed for negotiating these difficulties. When you have completed this task, share your work with your classmates. Then check the Appendix, and compare your lists to the ones we have composed. As a class, assess which items should be added to which list and why.

Notice that, like difficulties, strategies do not, can not, lead to single, uniform answers. This does not mean that the understanding they produce is chaotic, arbitrary, but rather that it reflects and is driven by each *different* reader's prior knowledge of subject matter, conventions, and ability to identify at least some of the cultural and educational forces constantly at work in his or her thinking.

Coda

Coda: A passage at the end of a movement or compo-sition that brings it to a formal close. [Lat. *Cauda* and Ital. *Coda,* "*tail.*"]

—*The American Heritage Dictionary*

Should you trace the definition of "coda" from the *American Heritage Dictionary* to *Dizionario della Lingua Italiana* by De Voto and Oli, you would find a long and interesting list of signifieds: as in a cat's tail, human hair tail (a braid), the tail of a tuxedo, and of a comet, but also, consequence, effect, musical background (music played as the list of a movie's participants scrolls on the screen), and finally, echo (prolongation of a sound due to its reflection on walls).

Of these, the **signifieds** that come closest to describing what we would like to focus on the most in these last paragraphs are the "consequence" and "effects" of the work done. We hope that, in your using of this book, you have developed a sense of trust in yourself as a reader of complex texts. That is: We hope the work you have done has taught you to trust that you have a repertoire of valuable knowledge, experiences, and pre-understandings that you can use as scaffold when tackling a new reading task. We hope you have learned to appreciate difficulties, recognizing and assessing them as signs of the work a text requires of its readers, as well as of the adjustments and revisions of a reader's knowledge they might call for. But above all we want this coda to sound as a celebration of your participation in a work of reading that began several years ago, with other students, whose texts echo in your interpretations, as they prolong and refract and weave together their voices with yours, and ours.

This time, we are at the end of our conversation: This book is approaching its conclusion, and by now you have learned to predict most of our moves. Keep these moves in mind. Surprise your teachers and us. Teach all of us to see how we can revise and enlarge our assumptions and assertions.

Glossary

Academic nomenclature *See* **discourse**.

Ambiguous/Ambiguity A term for multiple meanings, which at times seem to be at cross purposes. It is generally used to refer to something in the text itself; e.g., "this word is ambiguous." *See* **polysemy**.

Aura Literally, the atmosphere surrounding someone or something. Figuratively, the term is used to characterize the prestige of an author (i.e., Shakespeare's "aura"). Recognition of aura can both aid and interfere with how a reader negotiates a text. *See* **author function, negotiation.**

Author function A term used by Michel Foucault to refer to the reputation of an author. This reputation (much like an **aura**) is or becomes part of a reader's **pre-understanding** (prejudice, repertoire), creating expectations about how a text is to be read and interpreted. For Foucault, an "author" is not to be confused with the "writer," the totality of a flesh-and-blood human being.

Binary/Binarism/Binary opposition In literary study, the term is used to describe the relationship between two concepts, in which one is understood as antithetical to the other (e.g., good/evil). In a binary opposition, the concept listed first is considered normative in some way, while the second concept is its deviation or negation. For example, in the binarism "good/evil," good is privileged over evil—it is the standard by which evil is defined; thus, evil signifies the absence of good, or a turning away from it.

Canon "Canon" refers to a body of literary texts that, because of their unusually high aesthetic qualities, are presumed to have passed "the test of time" and thus merit considerable attention and study (Shakespeare's plays, for example). In recent years, the issue of "canon formation" has become a deeply contested one. Who decides which texts are or are not canonical? What constitutes "quality"? How do canons change, and why? What role is played by class, race, ethnicity, and gender in the formation of canons at particular historical moments?

Case study A **genre** popular in the social sciences. It is used to examine the experiences of individuals and groups, often providing evidence for or substantiating particular theories.

Close reading A strategy for reading texts that situates the "meaning" of a text in the words on the page rather than its historical or cultural contexts. Among its guiding assumptions are that texts are self-contained and self-explanatory and that readers discover meaning rather than construct it. *See* **context**.

Coded language Words and phrases (e.g., "boring") that may have rich and complex meanings for the writer, speaker, or group using them, but not for others. Such terms need to be explained, made explicit, unpacked. Coded language has the power to include (those who understand the code) and exclude (those who do not).

Commonsense A term used to refer to ideas that are taken for granted as obviously true and natural, as describing things as they are. It is a **discourse,** a way of interpreting and representing events and phenomena whose historical origins have been forgotten or are ignored. For example, we now accept as "commonsensical" the idea that every person is an unique individual, but that idea did not emerge until the late sixteenth century.

Context "Context" has varied and even contradictory meanings. It can refer to a text's historical, political, and cultural backgrounds, however defined. It can also refer to whatever ways a text can be "framed" (for example, psychologically or linguistically). Knowing, creating, or imposing a context can aid in the understanding and interpreting of a text. *See* **text** and **intertextual**.

Deep learning A learner's "active" production of knowledge; a learner's application or extension of prior understanding to a new context that generates new learning; revision and different understanding of prior knowledge.

Defamiliarize Derived from a Russian word that means "to make strange," the term was used by a group of theorists known as the Russian Formalists to describe the major purpose of art, which they believed is to restore freshness to perception by stripping away what has become familiar through habit. (Familiar things are not usually appreciated.)

Difficult/Difficulty Whatever is hard or challenging to understand in a text, for whatever reasons. A difficulty may impede the reading process at first, but it can also be a signal that our habitual ways of understanding might need to be revised, or that a different kind of interpretive work is called for. Sometimes a difficulty may appear "inside" a text; other times it seems a matter of a reader's lack of knowledge or experience. *See* **pre-understanding** and **repertoire**.

Discipline 1. A field of study, an academic specialization, in possession of a specific object of study, a shared set of problems, a common discourse. The purpose of a discipline is to produce knowledge. 2. Regulation. 3. Self-control.

Discourse A key term in contemporary theory. It can refer to: 1) a genre, e.g., dramatic discourse or the discourse of narrative fiction; 2) a kind of language, written or spoken, e.g., poetic discourse or prose discourse; or 3) the organized and systematic use of language within a discipline. A discourse can also be understood as a system of rules, implicit and explicit, determining who has the authority to speak within a particular **discipline** and what problems can be formulated and addressed.

Drama A literary genre characterized by impersonation, dialogue, and performance. For some theorists, all language, because it includes fragments of others' speech, has inherently dramatic dimension. Drama is performative. *See* **intertextuality**.

English Studies A term that is increasingly being used as a replacement for the academic study of "English" or "literature." It has the advantage of being more inclusive. Under its rubric are generally placed literary studies, composition studies, ethnic studies, race studies, gender studies, and critical theory.

Epigraph A quotation at the beginning of a book or chapter.

Event In narrative theory, it refers to a significant occurrence or action.

Fiction A familiar but slippery term. Currently, it tends to be used to distinguish imaginative writing from writing that is considered historical, journalistic, or "real-world," although each of these terms is also open to varied and contradictory renderings. The distinction between fiction and its opposite, however it is defined (*see* **binary opposition**), is likely arbitrary rather than innate.

Figurality/Figurative A term that refers to the evocative power of language, a power attributable to the functioning of metaphors or similar devices. For some literary critics, figurative language is understood as opposite to ordinary language (and thus is regarded as a kind of deviation). For others, all language is essentially figurative because it constructs rather than reflects reality.

Foreground To foreground an element of a text is to place it in a position to be noticed, to give it special attention. Conversely, a text's background is that which has been positioned not to be noticed, yet it functions like a backdrop.

Free verse Verse whose lines are irregular in meter and rhyme and are defined in terms of such principles as sentence structure and layout.

Genre A "genre" is a category, a type. To know the genre of a text is to be able to make certain predictions about it. *See* **hybridity**.

Graphic novel A type of text that resembles a comic book, but is more complex in its interaction of words and images.

Grand (or master) narrative A story a culture tells about itself. Often, a reassuring mechanism about the future; e.g., the "narrative of progress."

Hypothesis formation One's attempt and ability to discern the outcome of a narrative, a text's next move, the reasons for an author's choices, the rationale for a given position. Hypotheses are subject to revision.

Hybridity Another complex term with numerous applications. In this book, it is used to suggest that texts are not generically pure or consistent, but variegated. *See* **intertextuality**.

Image Language that appeals to the senses, especially sight. Language that is picturable. *See* **metaphor**.

Intention A term generally used to refer to a writer's sense of design, his or her purpose for writing. In recognition of the impossibility of knowing what a writer might really have been thinking (especially in light of psychoanalytical understandings of the unconscious, complex motivations, etc.), it has become commonplace to speak not of a writer's intentions but of a text's. A text's intentions can be identified through its foregrounded elements, repetitions, special emphases, and so on. To **read against the grain** is to read against this pattern of intention. *See* **text**.

Interpretive community A group of readers who, because of similar educational, cultural, familial influences, tend to read a text in similar ways, valuing the same or similar elements and assigning them the same or similar significance. An interpretive community may be synonymous with different theoretical schools (reader response, feminist, psychoanalytic) or different groups of readers within a given school. Interpretive communities are not fixed, but change over time. The term was introduced by the literary theorist Stanley Fish.

Intertextuality/Intertext The idea that any text is infused with memories, repetitions, transformations, and echoes of other texts.

Irony An indirect form of communication in which language is used to mean something different from what the writer seems to believe. The gap between words and belief is usually coded as something strange, disjunctive, or surprising.

Legitimize/Legitimation To "legitimize" is to grant authority (whether legal, social, disciplinary, religious, scientific, etc.) to an idea, concept, theory, practice, or behavior.

Literacy narrative A story generally told in the first person about the writer's acquisition of reading and writing skills.

Lyric poetry Brief poems that tend to emphasize the expression and analysis of emotion.

Meaning A most ambiguous word. While in this book, meaning is understood as resulting from a **transaction** between two **repertoires**—the reader's and the text's—other interpretive communities regard it as something discovered "in" the text. Behind these opposing conceptions are entirely different ideas about **text** itself. In the first instance, a text exists only *in potentia* (potentially) and requires active reading to be realized; in the second, it is something that exists autonomously, something into which everything of importance has already been poured (and thus requires "discovery").

Metalanguage The prefix "meta" is derived from the Greek for "above" and "over." A "metalanguage" (or metadiscourse) is any language that, from a higher, more abstract, level (over, above), comments upon language itself. It is also language that draws attention to itself as language.

Metaphor A figure of speech that refers to one thing in terms of another. Metaphors are understood as implicit comparisons, while similes, which use "like" and "as," are considered explicit. Personifications are a type of metaphor whereby intangible qualities or things are assigned human characteristics.

Multivocal *See* **discourse, polysemy**.

Narration A term used by Gerard Genette to refer to the filter through which what is read and abstracted is presented.

Narrative Poetry or prose that recounts events that can be arranged in logical and/or chronological or causal order.

Narrator The voice that narrates a text.

Negotiation A process, a strategy of give and take. In terms of thinking, or interpreting, negotiation suggests setting up possibilities, testing them, discarding, and revising them.

Paradigm A term originally proposed by Thomas Kuhn to refer to the framework of understanding that guides the process of scientific inquiry at a given moment in history. It is now used more broadly to refer to any framework of interpretation.

Persona *See* **voice**.

Personal essay A kind of writing often required in college courses, in which students are asked to write about an experience they have had. The "I" in such essays usually refers to the writer.

Personification *See* **metaphor**.

Poetry/Poetic discourse A **genre** or type of **discourse**. As genre, it focuses on the visual and musical elements of language; and it is divided into subgroups (such as lyric, ballad, sonnet), each with certain identifiable elements. As discourse, it is considered a type of language that **foregrounds** the linguistic properties of the **utterance**.

Polysemy Like "ambiguity," it refers to multiplicity. But it locates such multiplicity not only in a text's verbal elements but also "in" the reader or reading process. Unlike ambiguity, which can sometimes be clarified, polysemy resists resolution.

Prejudice *See* **pre-understanding**.

Pre-understanding Our minds are not blank slates. They house knowledge and understandings we are not always aware of. Although these *pre*-understandings can provide us with a base to begin a new task, they can also predetermine our moves and prevent us from entertaining new and different possibilities. *See* **difficulty, meaning**.

Propedeutic Preparatory. Introductory. Preliminary. The term suggests the need for preparatory steps but also the need to move beyond them.

Prose Often characterized as "ordinary" language, prose is considered more direct and straightforward than poetic discourse.

Reading Can be passive or active. Passive reading is a process of absorption. Active reading is a process of interpretation and reflection, whereby a reader constructs meaning, establishes significance, and reflects on the limits of his or her understanding. Active readers are often conscious of their moves and can describe them. In this book, a synonym for active reading is interpretation. *See* **close reading**.

Reading against the grain Every text indicates through patterns of emphasis and repetition how it asks to be read. To read against the grain of a text is to read against the system of textual directives, its apparent **intention**, and to explore alternative, even contradictory, possibilities.

Recursive reading A reading that returns the reader to a previously covered terrain. A deeper, more thorough, interpretation. (Connected to **hypothesis formation, negotiation, propedeutic**.)

Repertoire A reader's repertoire consists of the personal and academic experience, assumptions, and **pre-understandings** that he or she brings to a text and uses to shape an interpretation. But a text can also be understood as having a repertoire, which consists of its ideas, generic elements, techniques, forms, gaps, etc. It is the transaction between these repertoires that theorists such as Wolfgang Iser believe allows for the production of **meaning**. As Iser also explains, readers tend to approach a text in ways that will either confirm or challenge their pre-understandings.

Sign/Signified/Signifier This book draws its understanding of these terms largely from the work of the linguist Ferdinand de Saussure, who argued for the inadequacy of a referential theory of language (where language is believed to reflect a pre-existent reality). Saussure substituted for this theory one organized around the idea of "sign" as consisting of a signifier (word/image) and a signified (concept) that come into existence simultaneously (signifier is to signified as one side of paper is to the other). From Saussure's perspective, a signifier does not so much describe a concept as construct it. Saussure's theory of the verbal sign has been extended by other theorists to nonverbal signs, such as clothing (think of what is "signified" by different brands of jeans).

Simile *See* **metaphor**.

Story A term used by the narrative theorist Genette to refer to the chronological order of a text's events as constructed by the reader through process of abstraction and rearrangement.

Strategy (aesthetic) A method employed consciously and deliberately to define or solve an interpretive problem.

Subjectivity A highly complex term, which, in its simplest sense, can be said to refer to notions of identity as culturally and historically constructed.

Symbol Generally refers to anything that stands for something separate from itself: e.g., the American flag stands for patriotism; a white dove stands for peace. In literary texts, symbols are usually not so predictable—their meaning has to be inferred from a word's chain of associations.

System of notation and annotation Words and visual marks used by a reader to record responses during the reading process. Different **interpretive communities** may encourage readers to look for and privilege different kinds of elements while they read.

Text 1. Not to be confused with "textbook," it is a word that within literary discourse frequently substitutes for "work." While a work is assumed to be self-contained and autonomous, a text is thought to have boundaries that are both permeable and arbitrary; thus, text and context may be indistinguishable from each other in any absolute sense. While a "work" is assumed to be unitary, having a single meaning that it is a reader's responsibility to discover, a text is thought to have as many meanings as there are readers (or interpretive communities). Finally, while the term "work" is usually limited to literature, a text may refer to any system of signs, any effort at representation, whether a picture, poem, computer language, musical score, etc. 2. A term used by Gerard Genette in his discussion of narrative. It refers to the verbal representation of events in speech or writing, the spoken or written discourse itself, or what readers actually read.

Textbook A text that presents in a systematic and organized fashion the fundamental agreements of a discipline. It generally hides from view the history of those agreements and the controversies surrounding them.

Thesis statement Generally found in an academic essay, it consists of one or more sentences that attempt to establish the writer's main idea, purpose, problem, or question.

Tone The attitude to a subject or situation conveyed by an author or text through word, choice (diction), arrangement, and other elements. It is also used to refer to the mood a work engenders in its readers. *See* **voice**.

Transaction A term introduced into the field of reading theories by Louise E. Rosenblatt (who adopted it from John Dewey) to describe a way of reading in which neither text nor reader can be imagined or function without the other. *See* **negotiation**.

Utterance Unlike the sentence, which is a unit of language, an utterance is a unit of communication. Utterances are spoken, voiced.

Voice The impression a text creates that an author is speaking to us directly. "Voice" is often understood as equivalent to "identity" and "individuality." When a poem appears to be speaking to us in a voice we are not meant to confuse with the author's, the word **persona** ("mask") is used.

Works Cited

Abrams, M.H. *A Glossary of Literary Terms.* 6th edition. New York: Harcourt Brace, 1993.

Adams, Hazard. "The Difficulty of Difficulty." In *The Idea of Difficulty in Literature,* edited by Alan C. Purves, 23–50. Albany, NY: State University of New York Press, 1991.

Adams, Henry. *The Education of Henry Adams.* New York: Dover, 2002.

Barry, Lynda. *One Hundred Demons.* Seattle, WA: Sasquatch, 2003.

Berthoff, Ann E. *Forming/Thinking/Writing.* Westport, CT: Heinemann, 1988.

———. *The Making of Meaning: metaphors, modes, and maxims for writing teachers.* Westport, CT: Heinemann, 1987.

Bloom, Harold. *The Western Canon: The Books and School of the Ages.* Orlando, FL: Harcourt, 1994.

Calvino, Italo. *If on a winter's night a traveler.* Translated by William Weaver. New York: Knopf, 1993.

Coleridge, Samuel Taylor. *The Rime of the Ancient Mariner: Case Studies in Contemporary Criticism.* Edited by Paul H. Fry. New York: Bedford/St. Martin's Press, 1990.

Dandicat, Edwidge. *Krik? Krak!* New York: Vintage, 1996.

Derrida, Jacques. "The Law of Genre." In *On Narrative,* edited by W.J.T. Mitchell, 51–78. Chicago: University of Chicago Press, 1981.

Eco, Umberto. *The Limits of Interpretation.* Bloomington, IN: Indiana University Press, 1994.

Elam, Helen Regueiro. "The Difficulty of Reading." In *The Idea of Difficulty In Literature,* edited by Alan C. Purves, 73–92. Albany, NY: State University of New York Press, 1991.

Ellis-Fermor, Una. "The Nature of Plot in Drama." In *Modern Shakespearean Criticism: Essays on Style, Dramaturgy and the Major Plays,* edited by Alvin B. Kernan, 77–92. New York: Harcourt, Brace and World, Inc., 1970.

Emanuel, Lynn. *The Dig and Hotel Fiesta (Illinois Poetry Series).* Reprint edition. Champaign, IL: University of Illinois Press, 1994.

Foucault, Michel. "Death of the Author." In *The Norton Anthology of Theory and Criticism,* edited by Vincent B. Leitch, 1622–35. New York and London: W.W. Norton & Company, 2001.

Fish, Stanley. "Interpreting the *Variorum.*" *Critical Inquiry* 3 (1976), 191–96.

Gadamer, Hans-Georg. *Philosophical Hermeneutics.* Translated and edited by David E. Linge. Berkeley: University of California, 1976.

———. *Warheit und Methode.* Tubingen: Mohr, 1960. In English, *Truth and Method.* Translated by Garrett Barden and John Cummings. New York: The Continuum Publishing Corporation, 1975.

Genette, Gerard. *Narrative Discourse: An Essay in Method.* Translated by Jane E. Lewin. Ithaca, NY: Cornell University Press, 1979.

Heidegger, Martin. *What Is Called Thinking.* Translated by J. Gleen Gray. New York: Harper Colophon Books, 1968.

Hirsch, Edward. *How to Read a Poem: And Fall in Love With Poetry.* Orlando, FL: Harcourt, 2000.

Hynds, Susan. "Questions of Difficulty in Literary Reading." In *The Idea of Difficulty In Literature,* edited by Alan C. Purves, 117–140. Albany, NY: State University of New York Press, 1991.

Iser, Wolfgang. "Interaction Between Text and Reader." In *The Reader in the Text: Essays on Audience and Interpretation,* edited by Susan Suleiman and I. Crosman, 106–119. Princeton, NJ: Princeton University Press, 1980.

Johnson, Crockett. *Harold and the Purple Crayon.* Fiftieth Anniversary edition. New York: Harper Collins Juvenile Books, 1981.

Kuhn, Thomas S. *The Structure of Scientific Revolutions.* Chicago: University of Chicago Press, 1996.

Lentricchia, Frank, and Thomas McLaughlin, editors. *Critical Terms for Literary Study.* 2nd edition. Chicago: Chicago University Press, 1995.

Locke, John. Quoted in *An Enquiry concerning Human Understanding,* by David Hume. Edited by Anthony Flew. "Introduction," vii. Chicago: Open Court, 1988.

Mukařovský, Jan. "Standard Language and Poetic Language." Edited and translated by Paul L. Garvin. In *Linguistics and Literary Style,* edited by Donald C. Freeman. New York: Holt, Rinehart and Winston, 1970.

Miller, J. Hillis. "Narrative." In *Critical Terms For Literary Study.* 2nd edition, edited by Frank Lentricchia and Thomas McLaughlin, 66–79. Chicago: University of Chicago Press, 1995.

OED (Oxford English Dictionary) 1928 2nd edition. Edited by R. Burchfield et al. Oxford: Oxford University Press, 1989.

Owen, W.J.B., editor. *Wordsworth and Coleridge: Lyrical Ballads 1798.* 2nd edition. New York and London: Oxford University Press, 1969.

Peacock, Molly. *How to Read a Poem: And Start a Poetry Circle.* Toronto: McClelland & Stewart, 1999.

Pope, Rob. *The English Studies Book.* New York: Routledge, 1998.

Regosin, Richard. *Montaigne's Unruly Brood: Textual Engendering and the Challenge to Paternal Authority.* Berkeley: University of California Press, 1996.

Roethke, Theodore. *On Poetry and Craft*. Foreword by Carolyn Kizer. Poet Townsend, WA: Copper Canyon Press, 2001.

Rushdie, Salman. *Midnight's Children*. New York: Vintage, 2003.

Shakespeare, William. *Othello*. Edited by Russ McDonald. New York: Penguin Putnam, 2001.

Shakespeare, William. *King Lear*. Edited by Stephen Orgel. New York: Penguin Putnam, 1999.

Steedman, Carolyn K. *Landscape for a Good Woman: A Story of Two Lives*. New Brunswick, NJ: Rutgers University Press, 1987.

Vendler, Helen. *Poems, Poets, Poetry: An Introduction and Anthology*. Boston: St. Martin's Press, 2002.

Widdowson, Peter. *Literature*. London and New York: Routledge, 1999.

Further Reading

Bahktin, M.M. *Problems of Dostoevsky's Poetics*. Translated by R.W. Rotsel. Ann Arbor, MI: Ardis, 1973.

———. *Rabelais and His World*. Translated by Helene Iswolsky. Cambridge, MA: M.I.T. Press, 1968.

Barry, Peter. *Beginning Theory: An Introduction to Literature*. Manchester, U.K.: Manchester University Press, 1995.

Bartholomae, David, and Anthony Petrosky, editors. *Facts, Artifacts and Counterfacts: Theory and Method for Reading and Writing*. Portsmouth, NH: Boynton/Cook, 1986.

———, editors. *Ways of Reading: An Anthology for Writers*. 4th edition. New York: St. Martin's Press, 1996.

Belsey, Catherine. *Critical Practice*. London: Methuen, 1980.

Bleich, David. *Subjective Criticism*. Baltimore, MD: Johns Hopkins University Press, 1978.

Chatman, Seymour. *Narrative Structure in Fiction and Film*. Ithaca, NY: Cornell University Press, 1978.

Con Davis, Robert, and Ronald Schleifer, editors. *Contemporary Literary Criticism: Literary and Cultural Studies*. 3rd edition. New York: Longman, 1994.

Covino, William A. *The Art of Wondering: A Revisionist Return to the History of Rhetoric*. Portsmouth, NH: Boynton/Cook, 1988.

Culler, Jonathan. *Structuralist Poetics*. Ithaca, NY: Cornell University Press: 1976.

Donahue, Patricia, and Ellen Quandahl. *Reclaiming Pedagogy: The Rhetoric of the Classroom*. Carbondale, IL: Southern Illinois University Press, 1989.

Dubrow, Heather. *Genre*. London: Methuen, 1982.

Eco, Umberto. *The Role of the Reader: Explorations in the Semiotics of Texts.* Bloomington, IN: Indiana University Press, 1979.

Elbow, Peter. *What Is English?* New York: Modern Language Association and NCTE, 1993.

Epstein, Joseph, ed. *The Norton Book of Personal Essays.* New York: W.W. Norton and Company, Inc., 1997.

Fetterly, Judith. *The Resisting Reader: A Feminist Approach to American Fiction.* Bloomington, IN: Indiana University Press, 1991.

Freire, Paulo. *Pedagogy of the Oppressed.* Thirtieth Anniversary edition, with a new introduction by Donald Macedo. Continuum International Publishing Group: New York, 1993.

Gibson, Walker. "Authors, Speakers, Readers, Mock Readers." *College English* 11 (1950), 265–69.

Goleman, Judith. Working Theory: *Critical Composition Studies for Students and Teachers.* Westport, Connecticut and London: Bergin and Garvey, 1995.

Goring, Paul, Jeremy Hawthorn, and Domhnall Mitchell. *Studying Literature: The Essential Companion.* New York: Oxford University Press, 2001.

Graff, Gerald. *Professing Literature: An Institutional History.* Chicago: Chicago University Press, 1987.

Harkin, Patricia. *Acts of Reading.* Upper Saddle River, NJ: Prentice Hall, 1999.

Holland, Norman. "Literature as Transaction." In *What Is Literature?*, edited by Paul Hernadi, 206–18. Bloomington, IN: Indiana University Press, 1978.

Kameen, Paul. *Writing/Teaching: Essays Toward a Rhetoric of Pedagogy.* Pittsburgh Series in Composition, Literacy, and Culture. Pittsburgh, PA: University of Pittsburgh, 2000.

Kristeva, Julia. *Word, Dialogue, and the Novel.* In *The Kristeva Reader*, edited by Toril Moi, 35–61. New York: Columbia University Press, 1986.

Iser, Wolfgang. *The Act of Reading: A Theory of Aesthetic Response.* Baltimore and London: The Johns Hopkins University Press, 1978.

Iser, Wolfgang. *The Implied Reader: Patterns of Communication in Prose Fiction from Bunyan to Beckett.* Baltimore, MD: Johns Hopkins University Press, 1974.

———. "The Reading Process: A Phenomenological Approach." *New Literary History* 7 (1975), 7–38.

Lynn, Steven. *Texts and Contexts: Writing About Literature with Critical Theory.* New York: HarperCollins, 1994.

McCormick, Kathleen. *The Culture of Reading: The Teaching of English.* Manchester and New York: Manchester University Press, 1984.

McCormick, Kathleen, Gary Waller, and Linda Flower. *Reading Texts: Reading, Responding, Writing.* Lexington, MA: D.C. Heath, 1987.

Montgomery, Martin, Alan Durant, Nigel Fabb, Tom Furniss, and Sara Mills. *Ways of Reading: Advanced Reading Skills for Students of English Literature.* 2nd edition. London and New York: Routledge, 2000.

Newkirk, Thomas, editor. *Only Connect: Uniting Reading and Writing.* Upper Montclair, NJ: Boynton/Cook Publishers, 1986.

———. "Looking for Trouble: A Way to Unmask Our Readings." *College English* 46 (1984): 756–66.

Ong, Walter J., S.J. "Beyond Objectivity; The Reader-Writer Transaction as an Altered State of Consciousness." *CEA Critic: An Official Journal of the College English Association* 40 (1977), 6–13.

Palmer, Parker J. *The Courage to Teach: Exploring the Inner Landscape of a Teacher's Life.* San Francisco: Jossey-Bass, 1997.

Peters, John U. *The Elements of Critical Reading.* Upper Saddle River, NJ: Pearson Education, 1991.

Pope, Rob. *The English Studies Book.* London and New York: Routledge, 1998.

Rabinowitz, Peter J., and Michael W. Smith. *Authorizing Readers: Resistance and Respect in the Teaching of Literature.* New York and London: NCTE, 1988.

Richards, I.A. *Design For Escape.* New York: Harcourt, 1968.

Rosenblatt, Louise M. *Literature As Exploration.* Revised edition. New York: Noble and Nobel, 1968.

———. *The Reader, The Text, The Poem: The Transactional Theory of the Literary Work.* Carbondale, IL: Southern Illinois Press, 1978.

Salvatori, Mariolina. "Conversations with Texts: Reading in the Teaching of Composition." *College English* 58 (April 1996): 440–54.

———."Toward a Hermeneutics of Difficulty." In *Audits of Meaning: A Festschrift in Honor of Ann E. Berthoff,* edited by Louise Z. Smith, 80–95. Upper Montclair, NJ: Boynton/Cook, 1988.

Salvatori, Mariolina Rizzi. "Reading Matters for Writing." In *Intertexts: Reading Pedagogy in College Writing Classrooms,* edited by Marguerite Helmers, 195–217. Mahwah, NJ: Lawrence Erlbaum Associates, Publishers, 2003.

Salvatori, Mariolina Rizzi, and Patricia Donahue. "English Studies in the Scholarship of Teaching." In *Disciplinary Styles in the Scholarship of Teaching and Learning: Exploring Common Ground,* edited by Mary Taylor Huber and Sherwyn P. Morreale, 69–86. Washington, D.C.: Carnegie Foundation for the Advancement of Teaching and American Association for Higher Education, 2002.

Scholes, Robert. *Protocols of Reading.* New Haven, CT: Yale University Press, 1989.

Scholes, Robert, Nancy Comley, and Gregory Ulmer. *Text Book: An Introduction to Literary Language.* 2nd edition. New York: St. Martin's Press, 1988.

Seitz, James E. *Motives for Metaphor: Literacy, Curriculum Reform, and the Teaching of English*. Pittsburgh Series in Composition, Literacy, and Culture. Pittsburgh, PA: University of Pittsburgh Press, 1999.

Todorov, Tzvetan. "The Origin of Genres." *New Literary History* 8 (1976), 159–70.

Tompkins, Jane P., editor. *Reader-Response Criticism: From Formalism to Post-Structuralism*. Baltimore and London: The Johns Hopkins University Press, 1980.

Wiggins, Grant, and Jay McTighe. *Understanding by Design*. Alexandria, VA: Association for Supervision and Curriculum Development, 1998.

Appendix A

About Difficulties

A List of Difficulties

- Difficulties posed by readers confusing a text's surface with its depth (Chapter 1)
- Difficulties posed by a strangeness of content or formal arrangement (Chapters 2 and 6)
- Difficulties created by applying to a text expectations that do not "fit" (every chapter)
- Difficulties posed by a reader not knowing how to get started (Chapter 2)
- Difficulties posed by ambiguity (Chapter 2)
- Difficulties posed by unproductive assumptions such as "everyone has his or her opinion" (Chapter 2)
- Difficulties posed by tedium (Chapter 3)
- Difficulties posed by a text's historical remoteness (Chapters 3 and 7)
- Difficulties posed by knowledge transfer and hypothesis formation (Chapter 3)
- Difficulties posed by categories and binary oppositions such as "truth" and "fiction" (Chapter 5)
- Difficulties posed when a text cites material a reader has not read (Chapter 4)
- Difficulties created when one applies mechanical and uncritical assumptions about writing to reading, and vice versa (Chapters 5 and 6)

Strategies for Dealing with Them

- Annotating a text
- Playing with words (including consulting a dictionary and examining etymologies)
- Excavating your repertoire
- Identifying your pre-understandings
- Examining your reading and writing processes
- Using the Triple-Entry Notebook
- Writing about difficulty (the Difficulty Paper)
- Engaging in reflective questioning
- Trusting a response
- Testing a response
- Slowing down a reading
- Understanding a difficulty as something the text wants a reader to notice and account for
- Bracketing, highlighting some features before others, placing features in light and shadow
- Recognizing hybridity
- Trying not to do it all at once
- Understanding difficulties as opportunities, passageways to understanding, invitations to undertake particular kinds of work, *interesting* moments in a text

Appendix B

Two Poems by Robert Bly

Snowfall In The Afternoon

I

The grass is half-covered with snow.
It was the sort of snowfall that starts in late afternoon
And now the little houses of the grass are growing dark.

II

If I reached my hands down, near the earth,
I could take handfuls of darkness!
A darkness was always there, which we never noticed.

III

As the snow grows heavier, the cornstalks fade farther away,
And the barn moves nearer to the house.
The barn moves all alone in the growing storm.

IV

The barn is full of corn, and moving toward us now,
Like a hulk blown toward us in a storm at sea;
All the sailors on deck have been blind for many years.

Driving My Parents Home At Christmas

As I drive my parents home through the snow,
their frailty hesitates on the edge of a mountainside.
I call over the cliff,
only snow answers.
They talk quietly
of hauling water, of eating an orange,
of a grandchild's photograph left behind last night.
When they open the door of their house, they disappear.
And the oak when it falls in the forest who hears it through miles
and miles of silence?
They sit so close to each other…as if pressed together by the snow.

Appendix C

Carolyn K. Steedman

Landscape for a Good Woman

> The present tense of the verb *to be* refers only to the present: but nevertheless with the first person singular in front of it, it absorbs the past which is inseparable from it. "I am" includes all that has made me so. It is more than a statement of immediate fact: it is already biographical.
>
> (John Berger, *About Looking*)

Stories

This book is about lives lived out on the borderlands, lives for which the central interpretative devices of the culture don't quite work. It has a childhood at its centre—my childhood, a personal past—and it is about the disruption of that fifties childhood by the one my mother had lived out before me, and the stories she told about it. Now, the narrative of both these childhoods can be elaborated by the marginal and secret stories that other working-class girls and women from a recent historical past have to tell.

This book, then, is about interpretations, about the places where we rework what has already happened to give current events meaning. It is about the stories we make for ourselves, and the social specificity of our understanding of those stories. The childhood dreams recounted in this book, the fantasies, the particular and remembered events of a South London fifties childhood do not, by themselves, constitute its point. We all return to memories and dreams like this, again and again; the story we tell of our own life is reshaped around them. But the point doesn't lie there, back in the past, back in the lost time at which they happened; the only point lies in interpretation. The past is re-used through the agency of social information, and that interpretation of it can only be made with what people know of a social world and their place within it. It matters then, whether one reshapes past time, re-uses the ordinary exigencies and crises of all childhoods whilst looking down from the curtainless windows of a terraced house like my mother did, or sees at that moment the long view stretching away from the big house in some richer and more detailed landscape. All children experience a first loss, a first exclusion; lives shape themselves around this sense of being cut off and denied. The health visitor repeated the exclusion in the disdainful language of class, told my mother exactly what it was she stood outside. It is a proposition of this book that that specificity of place and politics has to be reckoned with in making an account of anybody's life, and their use of their own past.

My mother's longing shaped my own childhood. From a Lancashire mill town and a working-class twenties childhood she came away wanting: fine clothes, glamour, money; to be what she wasn't. However that longing was produced in her distant childhood, what she actually wanted were real things, real entities, things she materially lacked, things that a culture and a social system withheld from her. The story she told was about this wanting, and it remained a resolutely social story. When the world didn't deliver the goods, she held the world to blame. In this way, the story she told was a form of political analysis, that allows a political interpretation to be made of her life.

Personal interpretations of past time—the stories that people tell themselves in order to explain how they got to the place they currently inhabit—are often in deep and ambiguous conflict with the official interpretative devices of a culture. This book is organized around a conflict like this, taking as a starting point the structures of class analysis and schools of cultural criticism that cannot deal with everything there is to say about my mother's life. My mother was a single parent for most of her adulthood, who had children, but who also, in a quite particular way, didn't want them. She was a woman who finds no place in the iconography of working-class motherhood that Jeremy Seabrook presents in *Working Class Childhood*, and who is not to be found in Richard Hoggart's landscape. She ran a working-class household far away from the traditional communities of class, in exile and isolation, and in which a man was not a master, nor even there very much. Surrounded as a child by the articulated politics of class-consciousness, she became a working-class Conservative, the only political form that allowed her to reveal the politics of envy.

Many of these ambiguities raise central questions about gender as well as class, and the development of gender in particular social and class circumstances. So the usefulness of the biographical and autobiographical core of the book lies in the challenge it may offer to much of our conventional understanding of childhood, working-class childhood, and little-girlhood. In particular, it challenges the tradition of cultural criticism in this country, which has celebrated a kind of psychological simplicity in the lives lived out in Hoggart's endless streets of little houses. It can help reverse a central question within feminism and psychoanalysis, about the reproduction of the desire to mother in little girls, and replace it with a consideration of women who, by refusing to mother, have refused to reproduce themselves or the circumstances of their exile. The personal past that this book deals with can also serve to raise the question of what happens to theories of patriarchy in households where a father's position is not confirmed by the social world outside the front door. And the story of two lives that follows points finally to a consideration of what people—particularly working-class children of the recent past—come to understand of themselves when all they possess is their labour, and what becomes of the notion of class-consciousness when it is seen as a structure of feeling that can be learned in childhood, with one of its components a proper envy, the desire of people for the things of the earth. Class and gender, and their articulations, are the bits and pieces from which psychological selfhood is made.

*

I grew up in the 1950s, the place and time now located as the first scene of Labour's failure to grasp the political consciousness of its constituency and its eschewal of socialism in favour of welfare philanthropism. But the left had failed with my mother long before the 1950s. A working-class Conservative from a traditional Labour background, she shaped my childhood by the stories she carried from her own, and from an earlier family history. They were stories designed to show me the terrible unfairness of things, the subterranean culture of longing for that which one can never have. These stories can be used now to show my mother's dogged search, using what politics came to hand, for a public form to embody such longing.

Her envy, her sense of the unfairness of things, could not be directly translated into political understanding, and certainly could not be used by the left to shape an articulated politics of class. What follows offers no account of that particular political failure. It is rather an attempt to use that failure, which has been delineated by historians writing from quite different perspectives and for quite different purposes, as a device that may help to explain a particular childhood, and out of that childhood explain an individual life lived in historical time. This is not to say that this book involves a search for a past, or for what really happened. It is about how people use the past to tell the stories of their life. So the evidence presented here is of a different order from the biographical; it is about the experience of my own childhood, and the way in which my mother re-asserted, reversed and restructured her own within mine.

Envy as a political motive has always been condemned: a fierce morality pervades what little writing there is on the subject. Fiercely moral as well, the tradition of cultural criticism in this country has, by ignoring feelings like these, given us the map of an upright and decent country. Out of this tradition has come Jeremy Seabrook's *Working Class Childhood* and its nostalgia for a time when people who were 'united against cruel material privations...discovered the possibilities of the human consolations they could offer each other', and its celebration of the upbringing that produced the psychic structure of 'the old working class'. I take a defiant pleasure in the way that my mother's story can be used to subvert this account. Born into 'the old working class', she wanted: a New Look skirt, a timbered country cottage, to marry a prince.

The very devices that are intended to give expression to childhoods like mine and my mother's actually deny their expression. The problem with most childhoods lived out in households maintained by social class III (manual), IV and V parents is that they simply are not bad enough to be worthy of attention. The literary form that allows presentation of working-class childhood, the working-class autobiography, reveals its mainspring in the title of books like *Born to Struggle; Poverty, Hardship, But Happiness; Growing Up Poor in East London; Coronation Cups and Jam Jars*—and I am deeply aware of the ambiguities that attach to the childhood I am about to recount. Not only was it not very bad, or only bad in a way that working-class autobiography doesn't deal in, but also a particular set of emotional and psychological circumstances ensured that at the time, and for many years after it was over and I had escaped, I thought of it as *ordinary*, a period of relative material ease, just like everybody else's childhood.

I read female working-class autobiography obsessively when I was in my twenties and early thirties (a reading that involved much repetition: it's a small corpus), and whilst I wept over Catherine Cookson's *Our Kate* I felt a simultaneous distance from the Edwardian child who fetched beer bare-footed for an alcoholic mother, the Kate of the title (I have to make it very clear that my childhood was really *not* like that). But it bore a relationship to a personal reality that I did not yet know about: what I now see in the book is its fine delineation of the feeling of being on the outside, outside the law; for Catherine Cookson was illegitimate.

In 1928, when Kathleen Woodward, who had grown up in not-too-bad Peckham, South London, wrote *Jipping Street*, she set her childhood in Bermondsey, in a place of abject and abandoned poverty, 'practically off the map, derelict', and in this manner found a way, within an established literary form, of expressing a complexity of feeling about her personal past that the form itself did not allow.

The tradition of cultural criticism that has employed working-class lives, and their rare expression in literature, had made solid and concrete the absence of psychological individuality—of subjectivity—that Kathleen Woodward struggled against in *Jipping Street*. 'In poor societies,' writes Jeremy Seabrook in *Working Class Childhood*

> where survival is more important than elaboration of relationships, the kind of ferocious personal struggles that lock people together in our own more leisured society are less known.

But by making this distinction, the very testimony to the continuing reverberation of pain and loss, absence and desire in childhood, which is made manifest in the words of 'the old working-class' people that make up much of *Working Class Childhood*, is actually denied.

It would not be possible, in fact, to write a book called 'Middle Class Childhood' (this in spite of the fact that the shelves groan with psychoanalytic, developmental and literary accounts of such childhoods) and get the same kind of response from readers. It's a faintly titillating title, carrying the promise that some kind of pathology is about to be investigated. What is more, in *Working Class Childhood* the discussion of childhood and what our society has done to the idea of childhood becomes the vehicle for an anguished rejection of post-War materialism, the metaphor for all that has gone wrong with the old politics of class and the stance of the labour movement towards the desires that capitalism has inculcated in those who are seen as the passive poor. An analysis like this denies its subjects a particular story, a personal history, except when that story illustrates a general thesis; and it denies the child, and the child who continues to live in the adult it becomes, both an unconscious life, and a particular and developing consciousness of the meanings presented by the social world.

Twenty years before *Working Class Childhood* was written, Richard Hoggart explored a similar passivity of emotional life in working-class communities, what in *The Uses of Literacy* he revealingly called 'Landscape with Figures: A Setting'—a place where in his own memories of the 1920s and 1930s and in his description of similar communities of the 1950s, most people lacked 'any feeling that some change can, or indeed ought to be made in the general pattern of life'. All of Seabrook's corpus deals in the same way with what he sees as 'the falling into decay of a life once believed by those who shared it to be the only admissible form that life could take'. I want to open the door of one of the terraced houses, in a mill town in the 1920s, show Seabrook my mother and her longing, make him see the child of my imagination sitting by an empty grate, reading a tale that tells her a goose-girl can marry a king.

Heaviness of time lies on the pages of *The Uses of Literacy*. The streets are all the same; nothing changes. Writing about the structure of a child's life, Seabrook notes that as recently as thirty years ago (that is, in the 1950s, the time of my own childhood) the week was measured out by each day's function—wash-day, market-day, the day for ironing—and the day itself timed by 'cradling and comforting' ritual. This extraordinary attribution of sameness and the acceptance of sameness to generations of lives arises from several sources. First of all, delineation of emotional and psychological selfhood has been made by and through the testimony of people in a central relationship to the dominant culture, that is to say by and through people who are not working class. This is an obvious point, but it measures out an immensely complicated and contradictory area of historical development that has scarcely yet been investigated. Superficially, it might be said that historians, failing to find evidence of most people's emotional or psycho-sexual existence, have simply assumed that there can't have been much there to find. Such an assumption ignores the structuring of late nineteenth- and early twentieth-century psychology and psychoanalysis, and the way in which the lived experience of the majority of people in a class society has been pathologized and marginalized. When the sons of the working class, who have made their earlier escape from this landscape of psychological simplicity, put so much effort into accepting and celebrating it, into delineating a background of uniformity and passivity, in which pain, loss, love, anxiety and desire are washed over with a patina of stolid emotional sameness, then something important, and odd, and possibly promising of startling revelation, is actually going on. This refusal of a complicated psychology to those living in conditions of material distress is a central theme of this book, and will be considered again in its third section.

The attribution of psychological simplicity to working-class people also derives from the positioning of mental life within Marxism:

> Mental life flows from material conditions. Social being is determined above all by class position—location within the realm of production. Consciousness and politics, all mental conceptions spring from material forces and the relations of production and so reflect these class origins.

This description is Sally Alexander's summary of Marx's 'Preface to a Contribution to the Critique of Political Economy', and of his thesis, expressed here and elsewhere, that 'the mode of production of material life conditions the general process of social, political and mental life'. The attribution of simplicity to the mental life of working people is not, of course, made either in the original, nor in this particular critique of it. But like any theory developed in a social world, the notion of consciousness as located within the realm of production draws on the reality of that world. It is in the 'Preface' itself that Marx mentions his move to London in the 1850s as offering among other advantages 'a convenient vantage point for the observation of bourgeois society', and which indeed he did observe, and live within, in the novels he and his family read, in family theatricals, in dinner-table talk: a mental life apparently much richer than that of the subjects of his theories. Lacking such possessions of culture, working-class people have come to be seen, within the field of cultural criticism, as bearing the elemental simplicity of class-consciousness and little more.

Technically, class-consciousness has not been conceived of as *psychological* consciousness. It has been separated from 'the empirically given, and from the psychologically describable and explicable ideas that men form about their situation in life', and has been seen rather as a possible set of reactions people might have to discovering the implications of the position they occupy within the realm of production. Theoretical propositions apart though, in the everyday world, the term *is* used in its psychological sense, is generally and casually used to describe what people have 'thought, felt and wanted at any moment in history and from any point in the class structure'. Working-class autobiography and people's history have been developed as forms that allow the individual and collective expression of these thoughts, feelings and desires about class societies and the effect of class structures on individuals and communities. But as forms of analysis and writing, people's history and working-class autobiography are relatively innocent of psychological theory, and there has been little space within them to discuss the *development* of class-consciousness (as opposed to its expression), nor for understanding of it as a *learned* position, learned in childhood, and often through the exigencies of difficult and lonely lives.

Children present a particular problem here, for whilst some women may learn the official dimensions of class-consciousness by virtue of their entry into the labour market and by adopting forms of struggle and understanding evolved by men, children, who are not located directly within the realm of production, still reach understandings of social position, exclusion and difference. At all levels, class-consciousness must be learned in some way, and we need a model of such a process to explain the social and psychological development of working-class children (indeed, of all children).

When the mental life of working-class women is entered into the realm of production, and their narrative is allowed to disrupt the monolithic story of wage-labour and capital and when childhood and childhood learning are reckoned with, then what makes the old story unsatisfactory is not so much its granite-like *plot*, built around exploiter and exploited, capital and proletariat, but rather its *timing*: the precise how and why of the development of class-consciousness. But if we do allow an unconscious life to working-class children, then we can perhaps see the first loss, the earliest exclusion (known most familiarly to us as the oedipal crisis) brought forward later, and articulated through an adult experience of class and class relations.

An adult experience of class does not in any case, as Sally Alexander has pointed out, 'produce a shared and even consciousness', even if it is fully registered and articulated. This uneven and problematic consciousness (which my mother's life and political conviction represents so clearly) is one of the subjects of this book. A perception of childhood experience and understanding used as the lineaments of adult political analysis, may also help us see under the language and conflicts of class, historically much older articulations—the subjective and political expressions of radicalism—which may still serve to give a voice to people who know that they do not have what they want, who know that they have been cut off from the earth in some way.

The attribution of psychological sameness to the figures in the working-class landscape has been made by men, for whom the transitions of class are at once more ritualized than they are for women, and much harder to make. Hoggart's description of the plight of the 'scholarship boy' of the thirties and forties, and the particular anxiety afflicting those in the working class

> who have been pulled one stage away from their original culture and have not the intellectual equipment which would then cause them to move on to join the 'declassed' professionals and experts

makes nostalgic reading now in a post-War situation where a whole generation of escapees occupies professional positions that allow them to speak of their working-class origins with authority, to use them, in Seabrook's words 'as a kind of accomplishment'. By the 1950s the divisions of the educational establishment that produced Hoggart's description were much altered and I, a grammar-school girl of the 1960s, was sent to university with a reasonably full equipment of culture and a relative degree of intellectual self-awareness. Jeremy Seabrook, some eight years older than me and at Cambridge in the late fifties, sat with his fellow travellers from working-class backgrounds 'telling each other escape stories, in which we were all picaresque heroes of our own lives'.

But at the University of Sussex in 1965, there were no other women to talk to like this, at least there were none that I met (though as proletarianism was fashionable at the time, there were several men with romantic and slightly untruthful tales to tell). And should I have met a woman like me (there must have been some: we were all children of the Robbins generation), we could not have talked of escape except within a literary framework that we had learned from the working-class novels of the early sixties (some of which, like *Room at the Top*, were set books on certain courses); and that framework was itself ignorant of the material stepping-stones of our escape: clothes, shoes, make-up. We could not be heroines of the conventional narratives of escape. Women are, in the sense that Hoggart and Seabrook present in their pictures of transition, without class, because the cut and fall of a skirt and good leather shoes can take you across the river and to the other side: the fairy-tales tell you that goose-girls may marry kings.

The fixed townscapes of Northampton and Leeds that Hoggart and Seabrook have described show endless streets of houses, where mothers who don't go out to work order the domestic day, where men are masters, and children, when they grow older, express gratitude for the harsh discipline meted out to them. The first task is to particularize this profoundly a-historical landscape (and so this book details a mother who was a working woman and a single parent, and a father who wasn't a patriarch). And once the landscape is detailed and historicized in this way, the urgent need becomes to find a way of theorizing the result of such difference and particularity, not in order to find a description that can be universally applied (the point is *not* to say that all working-class childhoods are the same, nor that experience of them produces unique psychic structures) but so that the people in exile, the inhabitants of the long streets, may start to use the autobiographical 'I', and tell the stories of their life.

*

There are other interpretative devices for my mother which, like working-class autobiographies of childhood, make her no easier to see. Nearly everything that has been written on the subject of mothering (except the literature of pathology, of battering and violence) assumes the desire to mother; and there are feminisms now that ask me to return Persephone-like to my own mother, and find new histories of my strength. When I first came across Kathleen Woodward's *Jipping Street*, I read it with the shocked astonishment of one who had never seen what she knows written down before. Kathleen Woodward's mother of the 1890s was the one I knew: mothers were those who told you how hard it was to have you, how long they were in labour with you ('twenty hours with you', my mother frequently reminded me) and who told you to accept the impossible contradiction of being both desired and a burden; and not to complain. This ungiving endurance is admired by working-class boys who grow up to write about their mother's flinty courage. But the daughter's silence on the matter is a measure of the price you pay for survival. I don't think the baggage will ever lighten, for me or my sister. We were born, and had no choice in the matter; but we were burdens, expensive, never grateful enough. There was nothing we could do to pay back the debt of our existence. 'Never have children dear,' she said; 'they ruin your life.' Shock moves swiftly across the faces of women to whom I tell this story. But it is *ordinary* not to want your children, I silently assert; normal to find them a nuisance.

I read the collection *Fathers: Reflections by Daughters*, or Ann Oakley's *Taking It Like a Woman* and feel the painful and familiar sense of exclusion from these autobiographies of middle-class little-girlhood and womanhood, envy of those who belong, who can, like Ann Oakley, use the outlines of conventional romantic fiction to tell a life story. And women like this, friends, say: but it was like that for me too, my childhood was like yours; my father was like that, my mother didn't want me. What they cannot bear, I think, is that there exists a poverty and marginality of experience to which they have no access, structures of feeling that they have not lived within (and would not want to live within: for these are the structures of deprivation). They are caught then in a terrible exclusion, an exclusion from the experience of others that measures out their own central relationship to the culture. The myths tell their story, the fairy-tales show the topography of the houses they once inhabited. The psychoanalytic drama, which uses the spatial and temporal structures of all these old tales, permits the entry of such women to the drama itself. Indeed, the psychoanalytic drama was constructed to describe that of middle-class women (and as drama it does of course describe all such a woman's exclusions, as well as her relationship to those exclusions, with her absence and all she lacks lying at the very heart of the theory). The woman whose drama psychoanalytic case-study describes in this way never does stand to one side, and watch, and know she doesn't belong.

What follows is largely concerned with how two girl children, growing up in different historical periods, got to be the women they became. The sense of exclusion, of being cut off from what others enjoy, was a dominant sense of both childhoods, but expressed and used differently in two different historical settings. This detailing of social context to psychological development reveals not only difference, but also certain continuities of experience in working-class childhood. For instance, many recent accounts of psychological development and the development of gender, treat our current social situation as astonishingly new and strange:

> On the social/historical level ...we are living in a period in which mothers are increasingly living alone with their children, offering opportunities for new psychic patterns to emerge. Single mothers are forced to make themselves subject to their children; they are forced to invent new symbolic roles...The child cannot position the mother as object to the father's law, since in single parent households her desire sets things in motion.

But the evidence of some nineteenth- and twentieth-century children used in this book shows that in their own reckoning their households were often those of a single female parent, sometimes because of the passivity of a father's presence, sometimes because of his physical absence. Recent feminisms have often, as Jane Gallop points out in *The Daughter's Seduction*, endowed men with 'the sort of unified phallic sovereignty that characterises an absolute monarch, and which little resembles actual power in our social, economic structure'. We need a reading of history that reveals fathers mattering in a different way from the way they matter in the corpus of traditional psychoanalysis, the novels that depict the same familial settings and in the bourgeois households of the fairy-tales.

A father like mine dictated each day's existence; our lives would have been quite different had he not been there. But he didn't *matter*, and his singular unimportance needs explaining. His not mattering has an effect like this: I don't quite believe in male power; somehow the iron of patriarchy didn't enter into my soul. I accept the idea of male power intellectually, of course (and I will eat my words the day I am raped, or the knife is slipped between my ribs; though I know that will not be the case: in the dreams it is a woman who holds the knife, and only a woman can kill).

Fixing my father, and my mother's mothering, in time and politics can help show the creation of gender in particular households and in particular familial situations at the same time as it demonstrates the position of men and the social reality represented by them in particular households. We need historical accounts of such relationships, not just a longing that they might be different. Above all, perhaps, we need a sense of people's complexity of relationship to the historical situations they inherit. In *Family and Kinship in East London*, the authors found that over half the married women they interviewed had seen their mothers within the preceding twenty-four hours, and that 80 per cent had seen them within the previous week. Young and Willmott assumed that the daughters wanted to do this, and interpreted four visits a week on average as an expression of attachment and devotion. There exists a letter that I wrote to a friend one vacation from Sussex, either in 1966 or in 1967, in which I described my sitting in the evenings with my mother, refusing to go out, holding tight to my guilt and duty, knowing that I *was* her, and that I must keep her company; and we were certainly not Demeter and Persephone to each other, nor ever could be, but two women caught by a web of sexual and psychological relationships in the front room of a council house, the South London streets stretching away outside like the railway lines that brought us and our history to that desperate and silent scene in front of the flickering television screen.

Raymond Williams has written about the difficulty of linking past and present in writing about working-class life, and the result of this difficulty in novels that either show the past to be a regional zone of experience in which the narrator cancels her present from the situation she is describing, or which are solely about the experience of flight. Writing like this, comments Williams, has lacked 'any sense of the continuity of working class life, which does not cease just because the individual [the writer] moves out of it, but which also itself changes internally'.

This kind of cancellation of a writer's present from the past may take place because novels—stories—work by a process of temporal revelation: they move forward in time in order to demonstrate a state of affairs. The novel that works in this way employs contingency, that is, it works towards the revelation of something not quite certain, but *there*, nevertheless, waiting to be shown by the story, and the story gets told without revealing the shaping force of the writer's current situation.

The highlighting not just of the subject matter of this book, but also of the possibilities of written form it involves, is important, because the construction of the account that follows has something to say about the question that Raymond Williams has raised, and which is largely to do with the writing of stories that aren't central to a dominant culture. My mother cut herself off from the old working class by the process of migration, by retreat from the North to a southern country with my father, hiding secrets in South London's long streets. But she carried with her her childhood, as I have carried mine along the lines of embourgeoisement and state education. In order to outline these childhoods and the uses we put them to, the structure of psychoanalytic case-study—the narrative form that Freud is described as inventing—is used in this book. The written case-study allows the writer to enter the present into the past, allows the dream, the wish or the fantasy of the past to shape current time, and treats them as evidence in their own right. In this way, the narrative form of case-study shows what went into its writing, shows the bits and pieces from which it is made up, in the way that history refuses to do, and that fiction can't. Case-study presents the ebb and flow of memory, the structure of dreams, the stories that people tell to explain themselves to others. The autobiographical section of this book, the second part, is constructed on such a model.

But something else has to be done with these bits and pieces, with all the tales that are told, in order to take them beyond the point of anecdote and into history. To begin to construct history, the writer has to do two things, make two movements through time. First of all, we need to search backwards from the vantage point of the present in order to appraise things in the past and attribute meaning to them. When events and entities in the past have been given their meaning in this way, then we can trace forward what we have already traced backwards, and make a history. When a history is finally written, events are explained by putting them in causal order and establishing causal connections between them. But what follows in this book does not make a history (even though a great deal of historical material is presented). For a start, I simply do not know enough about many of the incidents described to explain the connections between them. I am unable to perform an act of historical explanation in this way.

This tension between the stories told to me as a child, the diffuse and timeless structure of the case-study with which they are presented, and the compulsions of historical explanation, is no mere rhetorical device. There is a real problem, a real tension here that I cannot resolve (my inability to resolve it is part of the story).

All the stories that follow, told as this book tells them, aren't stories in their own right: they exist in tension with other more central ones. In the same way, the processes of working-class autobiography, of people's history and of the working-class novel cannot show a proper and valid culture existing in its own right, underneath the official forms, waiting for revelation. Accounts of working-class life are told by tension and ambiguity, out on the borderlands. The story—my mother's story, a hundred thousand others—cannot be absorbed into the central one: it is both its disruption and its essential counterpoint: this is a drama of *class*.

But visions change, once any story is told; ways of seeing are altered. The point of a story is to present itself momentarily as complete, so that it can be said: it does for now, it will do; it is an account that will last a while. Its point is briefly to make an audience connive in the telling, so that they might say: yes, that's how it was; or, that's how it could have been. So now, the words written down, the world is suddenly full of women waiting, as in Ann Oakley's extra-ordinary delineation of

> the curiously impressive image of women as always waiting for someone or something, in shopping queues, in antenatal clinics, in bed, for men to come home, at the school gates, by the playground swing, for birth or the growing up of children, in hope of love or freedom or re-employment, waiting for the future to liberate or burden them and the past to catch up with them.

The other side of waiting is wanting. The faces of the women in the queues are the faces of unfulfilled desire; if we look, there are many women driven mad in this way, as my mother was. This is a sad and secret story, but it isn't just hers alone.

*

What historically conscious readers may do with this book is read it as a Lancashire story, see here evidence of a political culture of 1890–1930 carried from the North-west, to shape another childhood in another place and time. They will perhaps read it as part of an existing history, seeing here a culture shaped by working women, and their consciousness of themselves as workers. They may see the indefatigable capacity for work that has been described in many other places, the terrifying ability to get by, to cope, against all odds. Some historically conscious readers may even find here the irony that this specific social and cultural experience imparted to its women: 'No one gives you anything,' said my mother, as if reading the part of 'our mam' handed to her by the tradition of working-class autobiography. 'If you want things, you have to go out and work for them.' But out of that tradition I can make the dislocation that the irony actually permits, and say: 'If no one will write my story, then I shall have to go out and write it myself.'

The point of being a Lancashire weaver's daughter, as my mother was, is that it is *classy*: what my mother knew was that if you were going to be working class, then you might as well be the best that's going, and for women, Lancashire and weaving provided that elegance, that edge of difference and distinction. I'm sure that she told the titled women whose hands she did when she became a manicurist in the 1960s where it was she came from, proud, defiant: look at me. (Beatrix Campbell has made what I think is a similar point about the classiness of being a miner, for working-class men.)

This is a book about stories; and it is a book about *things* (objects, entities, relationships, people), and the way in which we talk and write about them: about the difficulties of metaphor. Above all, it is about people wanting those things, and the structures of political thought that have labelled this wanting as wrong. Later in the book, suggestions are made about a relatively old structure of political thought in this country, that of radicalism, and its possible entry into the political dialogue of the North-west; and how perhaps it allowed people to feel desire, anger and envy—for the things they did not have.

The things though, will remain a problem. The connection between women and clothes surfaces often in these pages, particularly in the unacknowledged testimony of many nineteenth- and twentieth-century women and girls; and it was with the image of a New Look coat that, in 1950, I made my first attempt to understand and symbolize the content of my mother's desire. I think now of all the stories, all the reading, all the dreams that help us to see ourselves in the landscape, and see ourselves watching as well. 'A woman must continually watch herself,' remarked John Berger some years ago.

> She is almost continually accompanied by her own image of herself. Whilst she is walking across a room or whilst she is weeping at the death of her father, she can scarcely avoid envisioning herself walking and weeping.

This book is intended to specify, in historical terms, some of the processes by which we come to step into the landscape, and see ourselves. But the *clothes* we wear there remain a question.

Donald Winnicott wrote about the transitional object (those battered teddies and bits of blanket that babies use in the early stages of distinguishing themselves from the world around them) and its usefulness to the young children who adopt it. The transitional object, he wrote, 'must seem to the infant to give warmth, or to move, or to have texture, or to do something that seems to show it has vitality or reality of its own.' Like clothes: that we may see ourself better as we stand there and watch; and for our protection.

A Thin Man

Roll up, roll up, come and see the mermaid,
See the lovely lady, half a woman, half a fish.
In went the lads to show it wasn't swank,
When little Tommy 'Iggins put some whisky in the tank.
Well, she got frisky, swimmin' in the whisky,
And when she come up for air
She bowed to the audience, gave 'er tail a swish;
'Er tail it come off, and she really looked delish;
She says, 'What d'y'want, lads, a bit o' meat or fish?'
At the Rawtenstall Annual Fair.

('Rawtenstall Annual Fair', 1932,
from Roy Palmer, *A Ballad History of England,* Batsford, *1979)*

By the time my father could sit down in a pub with me, slightly drunk, tell me and my friends about Real Life, crack a joke about a Pakistani that silenced a whole table once, and talk about the farm labourer's—his grandfather's—journey up from Eye in Suffolk working on the building of the Great North Western Railway, up to Rawtenstall on the Lancashire–Yorkshire border, I was doing history at Sussex, and knew more than he did about the date and timing of journeys like that. My father, old but gritty, glamorous in the eyes of the class of '68, a South London wide boy with an authentic background, described his grandfather's funeral, about 1912, when a whole other family—wife, children, grandchildren—turned up out of the blue from somewhere further down the line, where they'd been established on the navvy's journey north. (This was a circumstance paralleled at his own funeral, when the friends and relations of the woman he'd been living with for part of the week since the early 1960s stole the show from us, the pathetic huddle of the family of his middle years.)

When I look in the mirror, I see her face, but I know in fact that I look more like him. A real Lancashire face. He was a thin man. I knew his height, five foot ten, but he never seemed tall; he shrank in later years to not much above my height. The silhouette of men has changed completely since the 1950s, and it is this above all else that has altered the outlines of city streets; not the shape of the buildings nor the absence of trams and the growing sleekness of cars, but the fact that men no longer wear hats—broad-brimmed felt hats, tipped slightly over one eye. The Sandeman port man loomed on the hoardings outside Hammersmith Broadway station, the first thing I can remember, sitting up in my pram: an exaggeration and extrapolation of how they all looked, huge coat swirling, trousers flapping, the broad-brimmed rakish hat. A consistent point of my mother's propaganda against him was the shoddiness of his dress and the cheapness of his clothes, his awful ties, his refusal to spend money on his appearance, his lack of taste. But memory doesn't detail him like that; rather, a silhouette, a dapper outline.

*

He took me out once to a bluebell wood. My sister had just been born, we were waiting to move to Streatham Hill: spring 1951. I wore one of the two gingham dresses (I can't remember which colour, I can never remember the colour; they are both just the dress, the clothing of dreams). He was to take me out again, but this time in the bluebell wood was really the last time. I had a sister; we were about to move; his expulsion from the domestic scene about to begin.

It was shaded, a real wood, the sunlight outside beyond the trees, with a fern-covered slope up to the left of the path, the bluebells growing up the slope, and a clearing at the top of that. Up this small incline, and my father started to pick the bluebells from in between the ferns, making a bunch. Did he give me some to hold? I can't remember, except how else to know about their white watery roots, the pale cleanness pulled from the earth? And if he did give me some, what did I do with them in the next few minutes?

The arrival of the forest-keeper was a dramatic eruption on this scene, jarring colour descending on a shady place, a hairy jacket in that strange orange tweed that park-keepers still sometimes wear, plus-fours, brown boots and a porkpie hat. He was angry with my father, shouted at him: it wasn't allowed. Hadn't he read the notice, there'd be no bluebells left if people pulled them up by the roots. He snatched the bunch from my father's hand, scattered the flowers over the ground and among the ferns, their white roots glimmering, unprotected; and I thought: yes; he doesn't know how to pick bluebells.

My father stood, quite vulnerable in memory now. He was a thin man. I wonder if I remember the waisted and pleated flannel trousers of the early 1950s because in that confrontation he was the loser, feminized, outdone? They made him appear thinner, and because of the way the ground sloped, the forest-keeper, very solid and powerful, was made to appear taller than him. In remembering this scene I always forget, always have to deliberately call to mind the fact that my father retaliated, shouted back; and that we then retreated, made our way back down the path, the tweed man the victor, watching our leaving.

All the charity I possess lies in that moment. Any account that presents its subjects as cold, or shivering or in any way unprotected recalls the precise structure of its feeling. The child who told Henry Mayhew about her life as a seller of cresses in the winter of 1850 stands on the page clutching her shawl about her thin shoulders as the very aetiology of my pity. And there is a more difficult charity that lies somewhere beneath this structure, partly obscured by figures of the imagination like the little watercress girl: pity for something that at the age of four I knew and did not know about my father (know now, and do not know), something about the roots and their whiteness, and the way in which they had been pulled away, to wither exposed on the bank.

Summer came, and we started to live in the new house. It was June, a hot afternoon out in the garden, which was soon to become a farmyard of hen-houses and duck-ponds made out of old tin baths, but now on this hot day, a couple of weeks after we'd moved from Hammersmith, the perfect and sedate little garden made by the old couple who inhabited the house for forty years. The world went wrong that afternoon: there is evidence: a photograph. My father said 'Smile, Kay,' and I smiled; but it is really the day of my first dislocation. I lie on my stomach on the grass, my baby sister on a rug to my right, just in front of me. I am irritated and depressed because she has come to stay. Things have changed: on removal day I turned on the kitchen tap to fill a cup with water and couldn't turn it off, and the removal man was angry with me: the first time an adult's anger has been directed at me. I remember this now. Somewhere on the grass, beyond the photograph, is an apple that I've been given to cheer me up, but that I refuse to eat. We carry moments like this through a lifetime: things were wrong; there was a dislocation between me and the world; I am not inside myself. And he said 'Smile Kay,' and I smiled: the first deception, the first lie.

*

He had a story about how he left the North, a good story, well told. He'd had a few when he first presented it to me, and listeners from that Christmas meeting of 1967 in the pub remember its inconsistencies above anything else. The setting for the tale my father tells is the Blackpool Tower ballroom, it's the summer, and Robin Richmond is playing the organ. Which year? My calculation now says it must be 1934, but he doesn't mention dates himself. Is the famous organist introduced to add glamour to the occasion and the telling of it, even though my father affects to despise the sea-side medleys he's playing? Then suddenly Robin Richmond becomes a part of the story. My father implies that he's been carrying on with the organist's woman. Anyway, there's a woman somewhere in the story, a woman to fight over. There is a fight. On the dance floor or in the underground car park? It's unclear; but the story suddenly shifts to the car park anyway, and it's Robin Richmond punching him, and knocking him out; yet the music seems to go on playing.

Someone knocks my father out anyway, and he either gets into, or is pushed inside a car, on to the back seat. He has a lot to sleep off. The story cuts suddenly to South London, to Balham, and Ellis wakes up, not knowing where he is. The drivers of the car have brought him all the way from Blackpool, not realizing he's in the back. It's outside a lodging house, the car; the people are friendly. He eats bacon and eggs, 'looks around a bit', decides he 'likes the look of the place', borrows ten pounds, goes back North to 'collect a few things', coming back down again to the city in which he was to pass the next forty years of his life. He emphasized 'the few things': the phrase meant more than was apparent: one day, secrets might be revealed.

It's a good story, an allegory I think, that covers a plainer tale. Something had gone wrong, he was scared, he had to get out of town. Fifteen years after the telling, long after his death, looking at the suddenly revealed photograph on the bedroom mantelpiece, I found out what it was he'd left behind.

Underneath the Hammersmith flat, the flat we left in the early summer of 1951, was a cellar. It was part of the huge gothic building next door where he worked. It ran underneath our first-floor flat too, but to reach it you had to go down the stairs and out into the street first. Down here, my father kept his tools, and sometime during the year before we moved he started to make me a dolls' house. My mother took me down there to show me work in progress, the bare toy rafters and the little roll of tiled wallpaper for the roof. My father was surprised to see us, and in retrospect it is very odd that we should have made this descent, for later on, his not understanding the conventions of emotional life, like keeping surprises a secret—or preparing any sort of surprise, giving any sort of present—was to be one of the many items on my mother's check-list of his failures.

My mother leant back against a workbench, her hands on its edge behind her. It tipped her body forward, just a little. She leant back; she laughed, she smiled. Ellis stood under the spot of light, a plane in his hand, a smile: a charmer charmed. Years later it becomes quite clear that this was the place where my mother set in motion my father's second seduction. She'd tried with having me, and it hadn't worked. Now, a second and final attempt. By the time he took me to the bluebell wood, my sister was born, and our life was set on its sad course. The scene of seduction remained a mystery for a very long time, an area of puzzlement that failed to illuminate, like the light absorbing the darkness over the workbench. When I consciously thought about the mysteries of their relationship, I used in fact a highly literary set of devices.

My intensest reading of the fairy-tales was during the summer of my seventh year. The feeling of nostalgia and regret for how things actually are was made that June as Gerda in 'The Snow Queen' looked for Kay along the river banks that were eventually to lead to the queen's frozen palace, and she came to the place where the old woman, the witch, made all the rose trees sink into the dark ground so that Gerda would stay with her, not be reminded by the flowers of Kay, for whom she is searching.

Out the back, outside the room where the child reads the book, there grew a dark red rose with an ecstatic smell. The South London back gardens pressed up against the open window like a sadness in the dusk, and I lay on my bed, and read, and imagined what it was they were doing downstairs. The wireless was playing and I saw this picture: they both sat naked under the whitewood kitchen table, their legs crossed so that you couldn't really see what lay between. Each had a knife, sharp-edged with a broad yet pointed blade, and what they did with the knife, what the grown-ups did, was cut each other, making thin surface wounds like lines drawn with a sharp red pencil, from which the blood poured. In the book the Little Robber Girl whom Gerda has encountered on her journey north

> pulled out a long knife from a crevice in the wall and drew it across the reindeer's neck; the poor animal kicked with its legs, and the Robber Girl laughed and then pulled Gerda into bed with her. 'Do you take the knife to bed with you?' asked Gerda, looking somewhat scared at it. 'I always sleep with a knife,' said the Little Robber Girl. 'One never knows what may happen.'

Downstairs I thought, the thin blood falls in sheets from my mother's breasts; she was the most cut, but I knew it was she who did the cutting. I couldn't always see the knife in my father's hand.

In the same book, another girl, another woman—the Little Mermaid—longs to enter the world above the sea from which she is excluded by being what she is: 'More and more she came to love human beings, more and more she wished to be among them. Their world she thought, was far larger than hers.' It is love that will help her enter this world, desire for the prince whom she watches obsessively, as she swims round his ship, night after night. To enter this world of adult sexuality, to gain two legs instead of a fish's tail, she strikes a bargain with the Sea Witch: she must feel every step as if walking on the edge of knives, and her tongue must be cut out. In pain, dumb and silenced, she makes her sacrifice in vain, for the prince does not love her back; and when the day of his marriage to a mortal dawns, the Little Mermaid must die. Her sisters of the sea offer her the chance of life: by killing the prince and having his warm blood fall on her feet, her legs will join together again, into a fish's tail. But instead she sacrifices herself, flings away the knife, and is dissolved into the foam on the waves.

The fairy-tales always tell the stories that we do not yet know. Often, a few years later, I would long for my mother to get rid of my father, expel him, kill him, make him no more, so that we could lead a proper life. And what I know with hindsight about that summer of the fairy-tales, is that a new drama was in process of enactment. The removal of my father by the birth of my sister (an old, conventional story, every eldest daughter's tale) was being formalized by my mother's warfare against him, a warfare that always stopped short of banishment; and I was to end up ten, indeed twenty years later, believing that my identification was entirely with her, that whilst hating her, I was her; and there was no escape.

The Little Mermaid was not my mother sacrificing herself for a beautiful prince: I knew her sacrifice: it was not composed of love or longing for my father, rather of a fierce resentment against the circumstances that were so indifferent to her. She turns me into the Little Mermaid a few years later, swimming round and round the ship, wondering why I was not wanted, but realizing that of course, it had to be that way: 'How could he do it,' she said, 'leave two nice little girls like you?'

*

Our household and the registrar general's socio-economic categories mask a complicated reality. Social class is defined by a father's occupation, and during my childhood we must have belonged to class III (manual). A heating engineer without any training, he did get inside boilers and mend them, but more often told other men what to do. He was, in effect, a foreman. I think that for my mother, years before in the 1930s, her relationship with him had been a step up, a kind of catch for the weaver's daughter. His parents had once kept a corner sweet shop, and my mother told me when I was about eleven that they'd briefly had a pony and cart before losing it, and the business. She spoke of this vehicle, in which she'd never ridden, with a diffident pride: the little nod of pleased possession. But the pleasure had to be ambiguous now: she was already long engaged in revealing my father's meanness, vulgarity and lack of ambition. When he married in 1926 he gave his trade as traveller for a firm of mill-part manufacturers in York. There's a photograph that looks as if it were taken about this time showing a woollen mill decorated for Christmas, the girls turned towards the camera, their looms still, and standing amongst them one man, my father in a collar and tie, a visitor from the mobile world outside.

If we'd lived within my father's earning power, been uncomplicatedly his children, two meals a day round the kitchen table, parents sharing a bed (and the *car*; in all those years my mother was never driven anywhere in the firm's car) then our household would actually have represented, and represented to its children, the unambiguous position of the upper working class. But it was my mother who defined our class position, and the emotional configurations that follow on such an assessment. What is more, until we were in our thirties, my sister and I continued to believe that she bore the major burden of supporting us. As children we believed that without her we'd go hungry, and the knowledge of how little we cost came very late indeed.

He had nothing to give her in exchange for herself, not even the name that the statute books would allow him to bestow on her (and probably wouldn't have given it to her had he been able). The house was rented, the weekly seven pounds was payment for us, not a gift to her. She made us out of her own desire, her own ambition, and everything that came her way in the household was a by-product of our presence and her creation of our presence. We were an insurance, a roof over her head, a minimum income. We were her way of both having him and repudiating him. We were the cake that she both had and ate, before he left (though he never really left), and after.

In 1958 I passed the eleven-plus, and in August of that year the uniform I needed for grammar school was the subject of angry debate. He'd been approached for money for the gabardine mac, the tunic, the shoes, and he had handed some over, but not a lot. The uniform must have been a strain on the seven pounds. The issue, this Saturday afternoon, is the blouses that I will have to wear. I'm wearing a new one anyway, one from Marks & Spencer with blue embroidery round the collar, as I approach him at my mother's persuasion and drag his attention away from the form on telly. He asks why I can't wear the one I've got on. I'm profoundly irritated, outraged at his stupidity; they don't allow it, I say: it's a *rule*.

He did know some rules, but he didn't embody them: they were framed by some distant authority outside himself. For instance: I had become very timid in the years after 1951, often frightened of falling down, of appearing a fool. I disgraced him that summer in the public eye, sitting at the top of the slide on the Common, a queue of impatient children behind me, frozen with fear, quite unable to let go of the sides and slide down. In disgrace I turned round, made my shameful way down the steps again, the children parting in front of me and my father apologizing to the adults with them. He took me home and complained to my mother: there's something wrong with her, a child of five ought not to be frightened; a child of five ought to be able to slide.

He waited for me on the doorstep one time about a year later after he'd sent me down the road for a paper, because a neighbour watching me had said I was walking funny, looked flat-footed. I had my wellingtons on the wrong feet, it turned out. He knew the social prescriptions that said we ought to be alright, have *nothing wrong* with us—to be able to read, to walk straight—and that he was judged by our performance too.

In the mid-fifties he started to live in the attic, treated the place like a hotel. The firm put a telephone in the house, about 1956, so that he could deal with emergencies about burst boilers in the middle of the night. He came home at six o'clock, collected phone messages, made a mug of tea, washed, went out to his other life. Whilst we were children he always came back, sometimes before midnight. In the attic he read the *Evening Standard*, smoked a cigarette before he went to sleep. I interpret this nightly return as an expression of the ambivalent responsibility that lay in the seven pounds handed over on Friday, as a failure either to desert us or to change the situation he'd put us in: a man serving out his time, the maintenance payments as much a matter of obligation as those imposed in a bastardy order issued by a court of law. My sister says he came back because he didn't want to commit himself anywhere. He was a man of benevolent irresponsibility.

She wouldn't feed him, after about 1958, but he was allowed tea. Every morning in a red tartan dressing-gown he made his own. She must have bought the tea (that we were never permitted to drink) out of the seven pounds. Tea was tea and milk was milk (except for a brief flirtation with goats' milk, at which all the worms turned) but she had some choice over sugar, and refused to buy white poison. There was a long time, about 1960, when he complained every morning about the grittiness and how it made the tea taste. Later, I think he bought his own packets of Tate & Lyle.

We still had lodgers in the 1960s, not the glamorous turnover of the theatrical years, but sad, long-term men. My father met the newly arrived watch-mender on the stairs and said 'Hello, I'm the other lodger,' and the watch-mender believed him for days. This incident was remembered, given the status of a joke (our only family joke), an explanatory device, for my father to recall ten years later in the pub, for me and my sister to remember and laugh over after my mother's funeral. Curtailment of activity and exclusion from particular rooms of the house was a rule that my mother put into effect for all those men who handed over payment to her. The watch-mender wasn't allowed to use the bath—she said he was too dirty. This stricture didn't apply, however, to the Indian student who occupied the room before him. My mother explained that Hindus had to wash in running water and that they found us dirty. He had the charm of the exotic for her: anything foreign, over which she could show a classy tolerance, was a route away from her social situation. Later, she was to call herself a Powellite.

On Saturday afternoon the front room became briefly my father's territory. Racing on the telly, bets over the phone to the bookie, mugs of tea, whisky later on. He cleared the room after the football results and when he'd checked his coupon. This usage, I now understand, was his right within the treaty negotiated somehow with my mother. I could have read those rights in other actions, in the way, for instance, if he came home early on a weekday night and found us still in the front room, he'd switch off the lights, and fire and television, and leave us in the dark as he went upstairs to the attic; and in the permanently dismantled electric fire in my room, so that I could only ever burn one bar.

*

My father used to say: 'She's a wonderful woman, your mother,' or sometimes 'She's a bloody wonderful mother, Edna is.' When? When I asked him, on her instructions, for something. There was a long campaign, about 1961, to get him to buy a unit to replace the deep porcelain sink in the scullery (he didn't); pressure a few years later to get him to buy a house, and then to make a will. When I hear of passive resistance, I think of my father. All pleadings were now made through me. I would feel the justice of my mother's cause, raise the matter, usually Saturday lunch times after he got home from work, and before the racing started, plead the case, argue that she worked so hard. He never capitulated; listened; then: 'She's a bloody marvellous mother, your mother.' I can never read this deadly rejoinder, never, however many times I rehearse it, hear what it was he was saying. In interpretation it falls this way, then that; I don't know what he meant. It was a statement beyond irony (though it was ironic, in a way I couldn't and wasn't expected to understand: information withheld). He meant it in some way, revealed that he had surrendered to her interpretation of events, was playing the role assigned to him. Sometimes drink was mentioned: 'She doesn't drink, your mother.' I think the stories of maternal neglect brought from pre-War Lancashire expressed a reality that both of them knew about. Much later, he was genuinely shocked when, at twenty-seven, I wrote to my mother and said that I didn't want to see her for a while because she upset me so much. He said then that she'd been a good mother; but he'd forgotten the unassailable irony of fifteen years before.

There were fits and starts in their relationship, so dramatically altered at Christmas 1954. They got together again, the attic temporarily abandoned, about 1961. There were meals together; I remember weeping at Sunday dinner time into a bowl of tinned fruit, the tinned food itself a sure sign that some truce was being enacted. But it didn't last. Once, a dreadful time, the other life invading ours ('There's that woman on the phone again;' 'Why tell me?' 'Who else is there to tell?'), I packed all his things in the suitcases, and put them in the hall. I wanted him to go, for *something to happen*, something to change. I saw the future—work, the journey home, the quick meal, television, tiredness, my mother's life—stretching ahead for ever, like the long streets of South London houses; no end ever to be seen. But he didn't go. Nothing changed.

I still see him in the street, seven years after his death, a man of his generation, an old man at a bus-stop, his clothes hanging in folds; a way of walking. I shall never see my mother in the street in this way; she, myself, walks my dreams.

When he died I spent days foolishly hoping that there would be something for me. I desperately wanted him to give me something. The woman he'd been living with handed over two bottles of elderberry wine that they'd made together out of fruit gathered from the side of the ring road where her flat was. I drank one of them and it gave me the worst hangover of my life.

He left us without anything, never gave us a thing. In the fairy-stories the daughters love their fathers because they are mighty princes, great rulers, and because such absolute power seduces. The modern psychoanalytic myths posit the same plot, old tales are made manifest: secret longings, doors closing along the corridors of the bourgeois household. But daddy, you never knew me like this; you didn't really care, or weren't allowed to care, it comes to the same thing in the end. You shouldn't have left us there, you should have taken me with you. You left me alone; you never laid a hand on me: the iron didn't enter into the soul. You never gave me anything: the lineaments of an unused freedom.

Appendix D

Edwidge Danticat

Krik? Krak!

Krik? Krak! Somewhere by the seacoast I feel a breath
of warm sea air and hear the laughter of children.
An old granny smokes her pipe,
surrounded by the village children...
"We tell the stories so that the young ones
will know what came before them.
They ask Krik? we say Krak!
Our stories are kept in our hearts."

Sal Scalora, *"White Darkness/Black Dreamings," Haiti: Feeding The Spirit*

Night Women

I cringe from the heat of the night on my face. I feel as bare as open flesh. Tonight I am much older than the twenty-five years that I have lived. The night is the time I dread most in my life. Yet if I am to live, I must depend on it.

Shadows shrink and spread over the lace curtain as my son slips into bed. I watch as he stretches from a little boy into the broom-size of a man, his height mounting the innocent fabric that splits our one-room house into two spaces, two mats, two worlds.

For a brief second, I almost mistake him for the ghost of his father, an old lover who disappeared with the night's shadows a long time ago. My son's bed stays nestled against the corner, far from the peeking jalousies. I watch as he digs furrows in the pillow with his head. He shifts his small body carefully so as not to crease his Sunday clothes. He wraps my long blood-red scarf around his neck, the one I wear myself during the day to tempt my suitors. I let him have it at night, so that he always has something of mine when my face is out of sight.

I watch his shadow resting still on the curtain. My eyes are drawn to him, like the stars peeking through the small holes in the roof that none of my suitors will fix for me, because they like to watch a scrap of the sky while lying on their naked backs on my mat.

A firefly buzzes around the room, finding him and not me. Perhaps it is a mosquito that has learned the gift of lighting itself. He always slaps the mosquitoes dead on his face without even waking. In the morning, he will have tiny blood spots on his forehead, as though he had spent the whole night kissing a woman with wide-open flesh wounds on her face.

In his sleep he squirms and groans as though he's already discovered that there is pleasure in touching himself. We have never talked about love. What would he need to know? Love is one of those lessons that you grow to learn, the way one learns that one shoe is made to fit a certain foot, lest it cause discomfort.

There are two kinds of women: day women and night women. I am stuck between the day and night in a golden amber bronze. My eyes are the color of dirt, almost copper if I am standing in the sun. I want to wear my matted tresses in braids as soon as I learn to do my whole head without numbing my arms.

Most nights, I hear a slight whisper. My body freezes as I wonder how long it would take for him to cross the curtain and find me.

He says, "Mommy."

I say, "*Darling.*"

Somehow in the night, he always calls me in whispers. I hear the buzz of his transistor radio. It is shaped like a can of cola. One of my suitors gave it to him to plug into his ears so he can stay asleep while Mommy *works*.

There is a place in Ville Rose where ghost women ride the crests of waves while brushing the stars out of their hair. There they woo strollers and leave the stars on the path for them. There are nights that I believe that those ghost women are with me. As much as I know that there are women who sit up through the night and undo patches of cloth that they have spent the whole day weaving. These women, they destroy their toil so that they will always have more to do. And as long as there's work, they will not have to lie next to the lifeless soul of a man whose scent still lingers in another woman's bed.

The way my son reacts to my lips stroking his cheeks decides for me if he's asleep. He is like a butterfly fluttering on a rock that stands out naked in the middle of a stream. Sometimes I see in the folds of his eyes a longing for something that's bigger than myself. We are like faraway lovers, lying to one another, under different moons.

When my smallest finger caresses the narrow cleft beneath his nose, sometimes his tongue slips out of his mouth and he licks my fingernail. He moans and turns away, perhaps thinking that this too is a part of the dream.

I whisper my mountain stories in his ear, stories of the ghost women and the stars in their hair. I tell him of the deadly snakes lying at one end of a rainbow and the hat full of gold lying at the other end. I tell him that if I cross a stream of glass-clear hibiscus, I can make myself a goddess. I blow on his long eyelashes to see if he's truly asleep. My fingers coil themselves into visions of birds on his nose. I want him to forget that we live in a place where nothing lasts.

I know that sometimes he wonders why I take such painstaking care. Why do I draw half-moons on my sweaty forehead and spread crimson powders on the rise of my cheeks. We put on his ruffled Sunday suit and I tell him that we are expecting a sweet angel and where angels tread the hosts must be as beautiful as floating hibiscus.

In his sleep, his fingers tug his shirt ruffles loose. He licks his lips from the last piece of sugar candy stolen from my purse.

No more, no more, or your teeth will turn black. I have forgotten to make him brush the mint leaves against his teeth. He does not know that one day a woman like his mother may judge him by the whiteness of his teeth.

It doesn't take long before he is snoring softly. I listen for the shy laughter of his most pleasant dreams. Dreams of angels skipping over his head and occasionally resting their pink heels on his nose.

I hear him humming a song. One of the madrigals they still teach children on very hot afternoons in public schools. *Kompè Jako, domé vou?* Brother Jacques, are you asleep?

The hibiscus rustle in the night outside. I sing along to help him sink deeper into his sleep. I apply another layer of the Egyptian rouge to my cheeks. There are some sparkles in the powder, which make it easier for my visitor to find me in the dark.

Emmanuel will come tonight. He is a doctor who likes big buttocks on women, but my small ones will do. He comes on Tuesdays and Saturdays. He arrives bearing flowers as though he's come to court me. Tonight he brings me bougainvillea. It is always a surprise.

"How is your wife?" I ask.

"Not as beautiful as you."

On Mondays and Thursdays, it is an accordion player named Alexandre. He likes to make the sound of the accordion with his mouth in my ear. The rest of the night, he spends with his breadfruit head rocking on my belly button.

Should my son wake up, I have prepared my fabrication. One day, he will grow too old to be told that a wandering man is a mirage and that naked flesh is a dream. I will tell him that his father has come, that an angel brought him back from Heaven for a while.

The stars slowly slip away from the hole in the roof as the doctor sinks deeper and deeper beneath my body. He throbs and pants. I cover his mouth to keep him from screaming. I see his wife's face in the beads of sweat marching down his chin. He leaves with his body soaking from the dew of our flesh. He calls me an avalanche, a waterfall, when he is satisfied.

After he leaves at dawn, I sit outside and smoke a dry tobacco leaf. I watch the piece-worker women march one another to the open market half a day's walk from where they live. I thank the stars that at least I have the days to myself.

When I walk back into the house, I hear the rise and fall of my son's breath. Quickly, I lean my face against his lips to feel the calming heat from his mouth.

"Mommy, have I missed the angels again?" he whispers softly while reaching for my neck.

I slip into the bed next to him and rock him back to sleep.

"Darling, the angels have themselves a lifetime to come to us."

Between the Pool and the Gardenias

She was very pretty. Bright shiny hair and dark brown skin like mahogany cocoa. Her lips were wide and purple, like those African dolls you see in tourist store windows but could never afford to buy.

I thought she was a gift from Heaven when I saw her on the dusty curb, wrapped in a small pink blanket, a few inches away from a sewer as open as a hungry child's yawn. She was like Baby Moses in the Bible stories they read to us at the Baptist Literary

Class. Or Baby Jesus, who was born in a barn and died on a cross, with nobody's lips to kiss before he went. She was just like that. Her still round face. Her eyes closed as though she was dreaming of a far other place.

Her hands were bony, and there were veins so close to the surface that it looked like you could rupture her skin if you touched her too hard. She probably belonged to someone, but the street had no one in it. There was no one there to claim her.

At first I was afraid to touch her. Lest I might disturb the early-morning sun rays streaming across her forehead. She might have been some kind of *wanga*, a charm sent to trap me. My enemies were many and crafty. The girls who slept with my husband while I was still grieving over my miscarriages. They might have sent that vision of loveliness to blind me so that I would never find my way back to the place that I yanked out my head when I got on that broken down minibus and left my village months ago.

The child was wearing an embroidered little blue dress with the letters *R-O-S-E* on a butterfly collar. She looked the way that I had imagined all my little girls would look. The ones my body could never hold. The ones that somehow got suffocated inside me and made my husband wonder if I was killing them on purpose.

I called out all the names I wanted to give them: Eveline, Josephine, Jacqueline, Hermine, Marie Magdalène, Célianne. I could give her all the clothes that I had sewn for them. All these little dresses that went unused.

At night, I could rock her alone in the hush of my room, rest her on my belly, and wish she were inside.

When I had just come to the city, I saw on Madame's television that a lot of poor city women throw out their babies because they can't afford to feed them. Back in Ville Rose you cannot even throw out the bloody clumps that shoot out of your body after your child is born. It is a crime, they say, and your whole family would consider you wicked if you did it. You have to save every piece of flesh and give it a name and bury it near the roots of a tree so that the world won't fall apart around you.

In the city, I hear they throw out whole entire children. They throw them out anywhere: on doorsteps, in garbage cans, at gas pumps, sidewalks. In the time that I had been in Port-au-Prince, I had never seen such a child until now.

But Rose. My, she was so clean and warm. Like a tiny angel, a little cherub, sleeping after the wind had blown a lullaby into her little ears.

I picked her up and pressed her cheek against mine.

I whispered to her, "Little Rose, my child," as though that name was a secret.

She was like the palatable little dolls we played with as children—mango seeds that we drew faces on and then called by our nicknames. We christened them with prayers and invited all our little boy and girl friends for colas and cassavas and—when we could get them—some nice butter cookies.

Rose didn't stir or cry. She was like something that was thrown aside after she became useless to someone cruel. When I pressed her face against my heart, she smelled like the scented powders in Madame's cabinet, the mixed scent of gardenias and fish that Madame always had on her when she stepped out of her pool.

*

I have always said my mother's prayers at dawn. I welcomed the years that were slowing, [sic] bringing me closer to her. For no matter how much distance death tried to put between us, my mother would often come to visit me. Sometimes in the short sighs and whispers of somebody else's voice. Sometimes in somebody else's face. Other times in brief moments in my dreams.

There were many nights when I saw some old women leaning over my bed.

"That there is Marie," my mother would say. "She is now the last one of us left."

Mama had to introduce me to them, because they had all died before I was born. There was my great grandmother Eveline who was killed by Dominican soldiers at the Massacre River. My grandmother Défilé who died with a bald head in a prison, because God had given her wings. My godmother Lili who killed herself in old age because her husband had jumped out of a flying balloon and her grown son left her to go to Miami.

We all salute you Mary, Mother of God. Pray for us poor sinners, from now until the hour of our death. Amen.

I always knew they would come back and claim me to do some good for somebody. Maybe I was to do some good for this child.

I carried Rose with me to the outdoor market in Croix-Bossale. I swayed her in my arms like she was and had always been mine.

In the city, even people who come from your own village don't know you or care about you. They didn't notice that I had come the day before with no child. Suddenly, I had one, and nobody asked a thing.

*

In the maid's room, at the house in Pétion-Ville, I laid Rose on my mat and rushed to prepare lunch. Monsieur and Madame sat on their terrace and welcomed the coming afternoon by sipping the sweet out of my sour-sop juice.

They liked that I went all the way to the market every day before dawn to get them a taste of the outside country, away from their protected bourgeois life.

"She is probably one of those *manbos,*" they say when my back is turned. "She's probably one of those stupid people who think that they have a spell to make themselves invisible and hurt other people. Why can't none of them get a spell to make themselves rich? It's that voodoo nonsense that's holding us Haitians back."

I lay Rose down on the kitchen table as I dried the dishes. I had a sudden desire to explain to her my life.

"You see, young one, I loved that man at one point. He was very nice to me. He made me feel proper. The next thing I know, it's ten years with him. I'm old like a piece of dirty paper people used to wipe their behinds, and he's got ten different babies with ten different women. I just had to run."

I pretended that it was all mine. The terrace with that sight of the private pool and the holiday ships cruising in the distance. The large television system and all those French love songs and *rara* records, with the talking drums and conch shell sounds in them. The bright paintings with white winged horses and snakes as long and wide as lakes. The pool that the sweaty Dominican man cleaned three times a week. I pretended that it belonged to us: him, Rose, and me.

The Dominican and I made love on the grass once, but he never spoke to me again. Rose listened with her eyes closed even though I was telling her things that were much too strong for a child's ears.

I wrapped her around me with my apron as I fried some plantains for the evening meal. It's so easy to love somebody, I tell you, when there's nothing else around.

Her head fell back like any other infant's. I held out my hand and let her three matted braids tickle the lifelines in my hand.

"I am glad you are not one of those babies that cry all day long," I told her. "All little children should be like you. I am glad that you don't cry and make a lot of noise. You're just a perfect child, aren't you?"

I put her back in my room when Monsieur and Madame came home for their supper. As soon as they went to sleep, I took her out by the pool so we could talk some more.

You don't just join a family not knowing what you're getting into. You have to know some of the history. You have to know that they pray to Erzulie, who loves men like men love her, because she's mulatto and some Haitian men seem to love her kind. You have to look into your looking glass on the day of the dead because you might see faces there that knew you even before you ever came into this world.

I fell asleep rocking her in a chair that wasn't mine. I knew she was real when I woke up the next day and she was still in my arms. She looked the same as she did when I found her. She continued to look like that for three days. After that, I had to bathe her constantly to keep down the smell.

I once had an uncle who bought pigs' intestines in Ville Rose to sell at the market in the city. Rose began to smell like the intestines after they hadn't sold for a few days.

I bathed her more and more often, sometimes three or four times a day in the pool. I used some of Madame's perfume, but it was not helping. I wanted to take her back to the street where I had found her, but I'd already disturbed her rest and had taken on her soul as my own personal responsibility.

I left her in a shack behind the house, where the Dominican kept his tools. Three times a day, I visited her with my hand over my nose. I watched her skin grow moist, cracked, and sunken in some places, then ashy and dry in others. It seemed like she had aged in four days as many years as there were between me and my dead aunts and grandmothers.

I knew I had to act with her because she was attracting flies and I was keeping her spirit from moving on.

I gave her one last bath and slipped on a little yellow dress that I had sewn while praying that one of my little girls would come along further than three months.

I took Rose down to a spot in the sun behind the big house. I dug a hole in the garden among all the gardenias. I wrapped her in the little pink blanket that I had found her in, covering everything but her face. She smelled so bad that I couldn't even bring myself to kiss her without choking on my breath.

I felt a grip on my shoulder as I lowered her into the small hole in the ground. At first I thought it was Monsieur or Madame, and I was real afraid that Madame would be angry with me for having used a whole bottle of her perfume without asking.

Rose slipped and fell out of my hands as my body was forced to turn around.

"What are you doing?" the Dominican asked.

His face was a deep Indian brown but his hands were bleached and wrinkled from the chemicals in the pool. He looked down at the baby lying in the dust. She was already sprinkled with some of the soil that I had dug up.

"You see, I saw these faces standing over me in my dreams—"

I could have started my explanation in a million of ways.

"Where did you take this child from?" he asked me in his Spanish Creole.

He did not give me a chance to give an answer.

"I go already." I thought I heard a little *méringue* in the sway of his voice. "I call the gendarmes. They are coming. I smell that rotten flesh. I know you kill the child and keep it with you for evil."

"You acted too soon," I said.

"You kill the child and keep it in your room."

"You know me," I said. "We've been together."

"I don't know you from the fly on a pile of cow manure," he said. "You eat little children who haven't even had time to earn their souls."

He only kept his hands on me because he was afraid that I would run away and escape.

I looked down at Rose. In my mind I saw what I had seen for all my other girls. I imagined her teething, crawling, crying, fussing, and just misbehaving herself.

Over her little corpse, we stood, a country maid and a Spaniard grounds man. I should have asked his name before I offered him my body.

We made a pretty picture standing there. Rose, me, and him. Between the pool and the gardenias, waiting for the law.

Credits

Chapter 1, p. 12: "The Business" from *Collected Poems of Robert Creeley 1945–1975* by Robert Creeley. Copyright © 1983 The Regents of the University of California. Reprinted by permission of the University of California Press.

Chapter 2, p. 18: "One Art" from *The Complete Poems: 1927–1979* by Elizabeth Bishop. Copyright © 1979, 1983 by Alice Helen Methfessel. Reprinted by permission of Farrar, Straus and Giroux, LLC.

Chapter 2, p. 23: "Hands" from *Night Light* by Donald Justice, Copyright © 1967 by Donald Justice. Reprinted by Wesleyan University Press by permission of University Press of New England.

Appendix B, p. 138: "Snowfall in the Afternoon," from *Silence in the Snowy Fields.* Copyright © 1962 by Robert Bly and reprinted by permission of Wesleyan University Press. All rights reserved.

Appendix B, p. 138: "Driving My Parents Home at Christmas" from *This Tree Will Be Here for a Thousand Years, Revised Edition* by Robert Bly. Copyright © 1979, 1992 by Robert Bly. Reprinted by permission of HarperCollins Publishers Inc.

Appendix C, p. 140: *Source:* Steedman, Carolyn Kay, *Landscape for a Good Woman,* copyright © 1986, by Carolyn Steedman, Reprinted by permission of Rutgers University Press.

Appendix C, p. 140: Reproduced with kind permission of Virago Press, an imprint of Time Warner Book Group UK.

Appendix D, p. 168: "Night Women" © 1993, 1994, 1995 and "Between the Pool and the Gardenias" © 1993, 1994, 1995 by Edwidge Danticat, from *Krik? Krak!,* published by Soho Press, Inc., 1995, reprinted by permission of Soho Press, Inc.; all rights reserved.

Index